OPPORTUNITIES IN
VISUAL ARTS CAREERS

Mark Salmon

Foreword by
B. Martin Pederson
Publisher
Graphis Magazine

VGM Career Horizons
a division of *NTC Publishing Group*
Lincolnwood, Illinois USA

Cover Photo Credits:

Front cover: upper left, The School
of the Art Institute of Chicago;
upper right, Fashion Institute of
Technology; lower left and lower
right, Graphic Arts Technical
Foundation.

Back cover: upper left and lower
left, The School of the Art Institute
of Chicago; upper right, Graphic
Arts Technical Foundation.

Library of Congress Cataloging-in-Publication Data

Salmon, Mark, 1946–
    Opportunities in visual arts careers / Mark Salmon.
       p.   cm. — (VGM opportunities series)
    Includes bibliographical references.
    ISBN 0-8442-4031-1 (hardbound) — ISBN 0-8442-4033-8 (softbound)
    1. Art—Vocational guidance—United States. I. Title.
II. Series.
IN PROCESS

                                    92-18525
                                      CIP

Published by VGM Career Horizons, a division of NTC Publishing Group.
© 1993 by NTC Publishing Group, 4255 West Touhy Avenue,
Lincolnwood (Chicago), Illinois 60646-1975 U.S.A.
Manufactured in the United States of America.

2 3 4 5 6 7 8 9 0 VP 9 8 7 6 5 4 3 2 1

ABOUT THE AUTHOR

Dr. Mark Salmon received his B.A. from the University of Hartford, and his Ph.D. in sociology from New York University. He served as chairperson of the Humanities and Sciences Department as well as the Interior Design Department at the School of Visual Arts in New York City. He is also the former New York State commissioner (Downstate) of the National Association of Academic Affairs Administrators. Dr. Salmon serves as director of the National Conference on Liberal Arts and the Education of Artists, as editor of *Art & Academe: A Journal for the Humanities and Sciences in the Education of Artists*, and as codirector of the Institute for Visual Arts Research. He is the author of a number of articles on various aspects of the education of artists and designers. Dr. Salmon is currently academic dean at the Atlanta College of Art.

ACKNOWLEDGMENTS

The author wishes to thank the following individuals: Larry Anderson, Marshall Arisman, Linda Bastian, Virginia Beach, William Beckley, Lisa Beers, Stephanie Belcher, Christina Bertoni, Tim Binkley, David Campbell, Corrine Colarusso, Debara Farber, John Farkas, Lilly Filipow, Tom Francis, Pattie Belle Hastings, Allan Hing, Evelyn Hirata, Dolores Howard, Barbara Hutsell, Kay Kallos, Austin Kelly, Tom Klinkowstein, Chip Jameson, Bryan Jefferson, Bob Lobe, Janet Morley, Rene Price, Ned Rifkin, Mark Rokfalusi, Craig Scogen, Laura Seeley, Denise Sfire, Jay Shields, Libby Sims, Stephen Sinon, Jim Spruell, Ying Tan, Jan Taniguchi, Taresa Tantillo, Tommy Thompson, Elizabeth Turk, Shelly Unger, Seranda Vesperman, Norman Wagner, Bucky Wetherell, Elizabeth Wethersby, Richard Wilde, Jack White, and Robert Woertendyke.

In addition, I would like to extend a special note of thanks to Ann Chamberlain and Glenn Gritzer for their valuable help. I also want to take this opportunity to express my warm appreciation to David Rhodes.

FOREWORD

It is one of life's great challenges to find work that suits your temperament and makes the best use of your talents and education. If you are a visual artist, you may find the search for the right career especially daunting. The creation of art and design may seem far removed from the world of work.

If you do envision a career for yourself in the visual arts, remember that it is a demanding choice. The arts require talent, self-discipline, and tremendous love of craft and commitment. if you feel you have the ability, desire, and courage to succeed as an artist, this book is a good place for you to start. It explores the concept of fine art as a profession and examines the definitions, uses, and consequences of art. *Opportunities in Visual Arts Careers* will give you the practical information you need about the gallery system, sources of funding, and educational preparation. It will also help you research careers in the applied arts. Perhaps you will ultimately find your niche as a fashion designer, commercial illustrator, graphic designer, art director, or photographer. Or you might use your artistic ability to help educate or heal others through your work as an art teacher or art therapist. The visual arts offer a wide array of specializations as well as the opportunity to consider free-lance work or self-employment.

Good luck to you as you use this wonderful book to search for a way to turn your artistic aspirations into an inspiring career.

B. Martin Pedersen
Publisher
Graphis Magazine

INTRODUCTION

Imagine that you have been given an assignment by an art teacher. It asks you to find some free time—perhaps on a Saturday or Sunday—and to make a list of all of the "art" you can see in an hour. You go to an art museum and start to make your list. You move through the museum quickly and after an hour you have noted some 200 to 300 pieces of art—mostly drawings, paintings, and sculpture. Now, imagine that you are given another assignment by the same art teacher. This time you have the same basic task, but instead of going to a museum you are asked to find art at your local shopping mall. How much art will you see there?

You start out on you mission and as luck would have it, there happen to be several large prints of a well-known French Impressionist painter that have been used to decorate Macy's department store. The bookstore in the mall is also helpful for this assignment because it has some calendars for sale and each month these calendars feature the work of different artists. But that is about all you can discover. After an hour of looking, you cannot find any other works of art. Or can you?

If you expand your conception of what art is and take another look at the assignment, you will be able to find a great deal that can be regarded as art from an occupational point of view which does not necessarily fall into the same category as the paintings and drawings at the museum. What we are going to look at in our expanded idea of art is referred to as applied art, and there are many examples of this kind of work that we can find at a mall.

Let's start at Macy's. First of all, the lettering that gives the word *Macy's* its distinct look was created by an artist who specializes in that kind of design. Macy's distinctive lettering serves as a logo or company symbol. A logo may involve lettering, but it does not have to. Most of the stores in the mall have logos that have been designed by a graphic designer. In fact, virtually all large corporations have a logo that represents the company or its products. Such corporations as Coca-Cola, McDonald's, and AT&T all have logos that help identify the company and thus fix it in the mind of consumers.

But let's get back to the Macy's and the mall. Nearly everything that is related to the basic merchandising function of stores depends on such applied arts as graphic design, illustration, or photography. All of the packages for the products that you see in stores—packages that contain perfume, tennis balls, and candy—are all created by package designers. The clothing that Macy's and other stores sell is created by fashion designers. Household products of all kinds are created by industrial designers. The layout of the store itself, including the furnishings, the surface coverings on the walls and floors, the display areas and counters, and the lighting are all the result of the work of an interior designer.

If you shift your attention to the bookstore in the mall you will find that everything from book covers to the way in which the chapters are set up are the responsibility of designers. Book designers make use of photographs and illustrations to represent the ideas or events that the publication is attempting to convey. Similarly, magazines need photographers, illustrators, typographers, and graphic designers to make the images used in articles and stories. Magazines are also heavily dependent on designers who specialize in laying out the format of the pages. All of the advertisements that you see in magazines have been designed as well. Each time a new magazine comes out a designer will be hired to create a "look" for the new publication. When you open up a copy of *Time* or *Newsweek,* think about how much of what you see has been produced by artists.

These various logos, products, packages, clothing, books, magazines, photographs, and interior spaces are all very much a part of the world of commercial or applied art. They are also very much a part of the world in which we live. This idea will change the way you look at your surroundings and also the way you look at art. From this point of view, art is not simply something that is restricted to art museums and galleries. It is something that is basic to the experience of everyday life.

The next time you have cereal, toast, and juice for breakfast, look at the cereal box, the wrapping around the bread, and the carton of juice. A commercial artist has designed all three of them. In fact, when you go to the grocery store, nearly every surface you see—from labels on cans and bottles, to the display advertising for products, to the physical layout of the store itself—is the product of an applied artist. If you were to take away surface designs and images including lettering, much of your world would appear to you as an opaque shell. Once you have developed this kind of awareness you will realize just how often art touches each person's life every day of the week. You will also realize how dependent our culture is on the visual information produced by artists.

However, if you now begin to think of applied art as being essentially the same as fine art, you have missed the point. I do not mean to suggest that a painting by Rembrandt and the label on a jar of peanut butter are equivalent because clearly they are not. It is more correct to think of both of them as occupational areas that have much in common despite their differences. It is also true, however, that there are famous applied artists whose work is greatly respected in the art world and is represented in collections of some of the most important art museums in the world.

All of the work described above was produced by men and women who make a living as applied artists. Applied art, which includes design, has become one of the fastest growing and most important segments of our economy. One important reason for this is that good design has itself become a commodity that adds value to the things we buy. In addition, there has been a growing appreciation for the fine arts with more and more art galleries opening up around the country. It is not a surprise that the number of people entering the field of art and design is increasing. It is not easy to make a living in art and design, but for individuals with talent and determination the rewards are worth the effort.

CONTENTS

critics. Art styles and the art market. The market value of art. Educational credentials. Grants and other funding sources. Alternative sources of income.

CHAPTER 1

WHAT IS ART?

Anyone interested in pursuing a career should know something about the field that he or she would like to enter. With some fields, such as medicine, carpentry, or accounting, you probably have a reasonably clear understanding of what the occupational activity is all about. This is true, in part, because there is a good chance that you have been treated by a doctor, seen carpenters at work, and have had at least some experience in keeping track of your own personal finances, which is a simple version of what accountants do. However, you probably have had less contact with artists. What kind of people are they? What kind of work do they do? How do they make a living? How do people get a start in art? This book will help you to answer these questions and help you to see if a career in art makes sense for you.

If artists are people who produce art, then we want to start with a very basic question. What is art? This question yields a variety of answers. Perhaps the most direct answer and the easiest answer to understand, at least in its simplest form, comes from sociologists who would say that art is whatever people and institutions in society define as being art. If an art gallery, art museum, art college, or art critic call something "art," and if enough people in society accept their judgments, then by that definition, it *is* art. Such a conception of art, however, does not take the easy way out. Rather, it acknowledges a basic fact that is central to understanding art as a career: art is deeply embedded in the social institutions and cultural life of a society. In order to get a good grasp on the economic and occupational issues related to art as a career, we should adopt this pragmatic point of view.

You will find that art as an occupation is deeply connected to galleries, museums, private collections, art colleges, art programs in universities, art critics and magazines, corporate art collections, funding agencies, design companies, advertising and marketing, book and magazine publications, and a host of other social and cultural institutions. Art is sometimes discussed in highly abstract and conceptual terms. But in terms of career issues, it is advisable to take a very practical approach to the social networks and institutional contexts in which art is embedded.

TWO THEORIES OF ART

There are other practical conceptions of art as well. We will focus on two additional theories that also help set the stage for the focus of this book. First, art has been traditionally seen as a means to express the aesthetic ideas and feelings of the individual. In this view, art is defined as a means of aesthetic self-expression for uniquely gifted individuals. This is especially true of the art that has been produced during the last five hundred years up to the present. Art that was made during this period of time has been judged as the unique personal expression of each particular artist. The uniqueness and individuality of the artistic "genius" has been thought to be of primary importance for creative individuals. When we think of the great artists of the past, such as Michelangelo, Picasso, or Kandinsky, we are struck by how clearly we can identify their particular work. It has their individual creative stamp and we know it immediately by sight.

This uniqueness is especially characteristic of fine art works that involve drawing, painting, printmaking, and sculpture, as well as certain kinds of photography and work produced by electronic media. Fine art has often been concerned with producing individual works of beauty. Although the idea of art as being characterized by "beauty" may seem naive, irrelevant, or out of date by some contemporary artists, it is still a useful way to bring to mind a large range of fine art works that you might have already seen in books, museums, or galleries.

Today's fine artists are oftentimes more concerned with representing a wide range of abstract ideas and or social ideals in their work than they are in producing works of beauty. This particular approach to art is not new. In fact, the opposing views of art purely as an expression of aesthetic ideals versus art as social commentary and criticism have been around since the nineteenth century and continue to be represented in the art world.

The concern with aesthetic self-expression has contributed to the somewhat ambiguous role of the artist in modern society. On the one hand, artists who have wanted to earn a living through their art have had to be sensitive to the values and taste of the public. On the other hand, they have also been preoccupied with pursuing a very personal artistic vision that, for a variety of reasons, has sometimes been insensitive to social standards.

Thus, occasionally there is tension between artistic expression and public acceptance of art. This is especially true in a democratic society where individualism creates the possibility of many artistic points of view. As artists engage the values and issues of their time, they may produce art that is controversial, inflammatory, or contrary to social standards. In those cases, artists may receive less support for their work from critics, patrons, and agencies than artists whose work falls within a broad range of what is typically regarded as acceptable. Issues over the public funding of controversial art testify to this occasional tension between personal aesthetics and public values.

Striking a balance between personal artistic vision and broader public taste can be a significant occupational issue for artists. However, an artist who continues to produce work that no one wants to buy may derive personal satisfaction from the work that he or she produces, but will have a difficult time sharing that satisfaction with a consuming public. Today's artists are quite sensitive to public taste and the marketability of their work. In fact, that has become so much the case that successful artists are occasionally suspected of compromising meaningful aesthetic standards for the sake of financial success. However, it is sometimes those artists who cannot sell their work and alienated intellectuals who raise these kinds of questions.

The second basic definition of art focuses less on creative expression and more on the usefulness of art. Since the earliest days of human history, art has had a practical role in serving the needs of people in society. Thousands of years ago, for example, the earliest human beings painted pictures of animals on caves. Some art historians think that they did so as part of a magical ritual that would help them tame animal "spirits" thereby making their prey easier to hunt. Therefore, to get a full picture of the history of art you need to remember that art has often been used for a variety of practical purposes. It has been used to express ideas, convey information, or design products that people use on a daily basis. Aesthetic concerns are still present in these works, but they are merged with and sometimes subordinate to a variety of functional considerations.

Some eight or nine hundred years ago during the Middle Ages art was considered to be a practical occupation. Art was not thought of in terms of unique creative genius, but was considered to be a craft very much like other crafts, such as smithery, weaving, carpentry, or shoemaking. Artists of that period were regarded simply as manual laborers and would typically work as building designers, sign painters, or book illustrators. Practical considerations have continued to be an important part of the craft tradition of art.

Today, art that has a practical purpose is sometimes referred to as commercial art, but artists who produce this kind of work usually prefer to use the term *applied art*. Because certain kinds of applied art such as fashion design or graphic design are intended to be useful, they have not had the same history of antagonism with public taste as with some fine art. This does not mean that the taste of the consuming public has not exerted pressure on applied artists. The public has often expressed a clear preference for particular design characteristics of the applied arts just as it has with fine art. The fundamental difference, however, is that the applied artists belong to an occupational tradition that has sought to respond to and satisfy public taste, whereas fine artists belong to an occupational tradition that in the last century has often been indifferent and sometimes antagonistic to public taste. Differences in attitudes toward public taste on the part of fine and applied artists are part of a larger set of issues that have made an impact of the economics of art.

THE CREATIVE LINK

As a result of the two traditions that are outlined above, the world of art essentially falls into either the category of fine art or applied art. Fine art includes the kind of paintings, drawings, or sculpture that you might find in your local art museum or art gallery. It is what most people think of first when they think of "art." Fine art is evaluated in terms of criteria related to personal creativity and aesthetics as well as visual and thematic relevance. Because contemporary art is sometimes intended as political critique or social comment, it has increasingly taken on a practical role related to social transformation. There have been similar practical uses of fine art that have made some artists and critics uncomfortable. The official art of the former Soviet Union and its use as propaganda would be an example. It remains true, however, that most fine art is still guided by aesthetic standards that generally avoid practical considerations.

Applied art involves a wide range of work that is largely but not exclusively concerned with design. The applied arts include such fields as illustration, advertising design, graphic design, fashion design, and interior design. While aesthetic issues are still considered to be very important and have actually been the motivating force behind some important design movements, they are usually seen as enhancing rather than defining the underlying practical value of the applied arts.

That added value is important and should not be taken for granted. This is because good design does more than simply add an aesthetic dimension to our everyday world. It can also make that world an easier, safer, and more satisfying place in which to live, work, and play. In addition, good design can influence our ability to recognize culturally and economically significant objects and ideas. Therefore, the visual element in design adds value to our everyday world.

Thus, the fine and applied arts share much in common. Aesthetics are important to both fine and applied arts. As we have seen, aesthetic issues define fine art. Forms of personal expression are usually only defined as art when they satisfy some basic aesthetic criterion such as "beauty" or "social truth." But aesthetics are also important to the applied arts. This is true because while the applied arts produce a useful product, they are created with a strong sense of good design. The aesthetic impulse of designers and the useful function of what they produce actually complement one another. They do so because good design has become as important a part of the marketability of products as their functional values. People are no longer content to limit their aesthetic experiences to what they see at an art museum. They now want to surround themselves with good design and to make aesthetic experiences a part of their everyday lives. Automotive companies and clothing manufacturers have known this for a long time. Today the producers of nearly all consumer products understand it as well.

Because aesthetics are important to the fine and applied arts, they are both the creative extensions of the individual artist or designer. Creativity grows out of an impulse that emerges from within the individual. This is something that all artists and designers experience intensely and enjoy deeply. If you are currently involved in drawing, painting, photography, or some other form of art, you very well may have experienced this creative impulse yourself. The satisfaction that comes from being creative and from living the creative life is an important part of what makes art so fulfilling from an occupational point of view.

Another significant link between fine artists and applied artists is that they are both trained in art colleges or in art programs in universities, and share a similar or overlapping curriculum. In fact, students who major in painting, sculpture, graphic design, and illustration will typically have a common first-year curriculum. Fine and applied art students will often be in classes with one another and the exposure can be of value to both of them. Fine and applied art students may also have basic technologies in common such as cameras, computers, or video. In addition, faculty who teach fine art courses may teach in an applied art area as well.

One reason that the curricular content for fine and applied students can overlap to the extent that it does is because there are common issues that they both must address in their work. All artists—both fine and applied—face basic aesthetic problems related to line, color, composition, scale, content, concept development, and creative vision, as well as artistic concerns related to materials and techniques. These elements form the basic visual vocabulary and technical foundation of art, whether it be advertising design, illustration, or sculpture.

Another important link between fine and applied art is that they both reflect the experiences of artists who live and work in a particular cultural period. Artists who belong to an historical period within a society will be exposed to similar cultural experiences that shape consciousness and artistic vision. When various artists produce their own unique expression of common cultural experiences, the result is the development of a particular style or period in art. It is because of the impact of culture on individual experience that artistic works within a style or period have something in common. This suggests an interesting role for the artist in society. Presumably all individuals in society will be exposed to a similar set of basic experiences, yet only artists seem able to translate those experiences into images that others can appreciate on an aesthetic level. In that way, all artists are able to bridge the gap between the external reality of the everyday world and the subjective aesthetic experience of artistic contemplation.

From an occupational point of view, the nature, structure, and conditions of the work of fine and applied art may also have much in common. This is especially true for applied artists who do free-lance work. Both fine artists and free-lance applied artists are in business for themselves and must conduct many aspects of their professional lives on that basis. In addition, it is sometimes the case that an individual may begin with a focus on one kind of art early in his or her career only to shift to another kind of art later on. Moreover, each kind of artist may also be influenced by, borrow from, or be interrelated with the other kind of artist. In fact, there are a variety of important connections and elements in common between fine art and commercial art. The point, however, is not to argue the ways in which fine and applied art are alike or different, but rather to make the general point that the term "art" is broad enough to include them both.

CHAPTER 2

MAKING ART

Artists are people who produce art. Therefore, we should consider how art is produced as a preliminary step that will give us insight into the occupational aspects of art as a career. Understanding how art is made is not necessarily the same thing as learning how an artist thinks, feels, and acts during the creative process. It can also involve understanding the other elements that contribute to the artistic process and how that process is developed.

The artistic process can vary to a considerable degree. There are perhaps as many styles of working as there are styles of art. This is what one might expect of such a highly individualistic endeavor. Some artists work at night and some during the day. Some need music for inspiration while they produce, others prefer the reassuring calm of silence. Some artists get their ideas directly from life and some rely on their imaginations.

Despite those differences, however, there are some common elements in the process of making art that most successful artists share. The key word here is *successful*. As in other fields, success in art is the result of hard work as much as it is the result of talent. Only some of the individuals who attempt to make art a career succeed. There are those who make fleeting and half-hearted efforts at being artists, but these people fall by the wayside quickly. Success, however, need not necessarily be measured in terms of career issues only. It can also be measured by such things as personal growth and self-discovery. The sections that follow do not provide a formula for a great career in art or design, but they are important ingredients and they should be considered carefully.

A COMMITMENT TO ART

Some elements that contribute to success in art are hard to measure, and one of them is commitment. Commitment to art involves a highly motivated orientation toward one's future. It is based on several things. An important one is the love of art. It does not make sense to consider pursuing art as a career unless you really like to make art. The joy of art and the art-making process are important aspects of the psychological rewards of the profession.

As you consider whether to go into art, ask yourself this simple question, "How important is it for me to make art, and how often do I make it?" If you enjoy art but don't like to produce it, then perhaps you might want to consider becoming an art historian, art critic, or art dealer. Or, if you make art but don't really like doing it, you may be going through the motions to make someone else happy. In either case, you will probably not be able to develop the genuine commitment you need to become a successful artist.

Commitment to art is sustained not only by the love of art, but also by the various rewards that involvement in art can provide. Those rewards can be both internal (the satisfaction of making art) and external (the professional rewards that come with career success). This book is devoted to understanding the many career opportunities in the visual arts that make it personally as well as professionally rewarding.

A commitment to art really means the willingness to pursue long-range goals. One of the characteristics of the professions that we will look at in Chapter 3 is that they involve a lengthy period of training. That training can begin at an early age. For example, you may have enjoyed playing with crayons or finger paints as a child. Or you might have become involved with art in high school. Whenever you start, you must be willing to stay with it. The willingness to work toward a future goal is also an important part of a commitment to art.

Unlike the world of music in which children can become prodigies at an early age, there have not been very many people who have been successful artists without much artistic training and a great deal of experience making art. Therefore, you must understand that there may be a considerable period of time before you become accomplished enough to make your art career pay off. Some artists are fortunate enough to begin to develop successful careers during or right after attending art college. For others, it takes a combination of time, hard work, and some aggressive entrepreneurial know-how.

HARD WORK

Of all the ingredients, perhaps the single most important one that contributes to doing well in the field of art and design is hard work. That idea should be obvious, but unfortunately it is sometimes obscured by naive images of the bohemian artist. Artists have sometimes been thought of as being lazy and self-indulgent. In addition, there is a tradition in western culture that has associated creativity with play. We sometimes speak, for example, of "playing with a new idea." Thinking of art as the product of lazy or playful bohemians is an unfortunate stereotype that was perhaps created by people who went off to work in the morning, put in a hard day at their job, and came home tired at night. From their point of view, staying in an artist's studio and painting, drawing, or sculpting is not work.

But they are quite mistaken. Making art does require hard work and long hours. Hard work involves sustained concentration and the fully conscious involvement of one's self in activities. At the end of the day artists and designers often feel both deeply satisfied and very tired. If you want to pursue art as a career, you must be prepared to work long and hard to achieve your professional objectives. If you are thinking about applying to an art college or to an art program in a university, you need to understand what lies ahead and begin to develop good work habits right now, not only in art but in all of your academic subjects. The application procedure to art colleges and art programs in universities will be discussed in detail in subsequent chapters of this book.

SELF-DISCIPLINE

If you were to become employed by a design company, you would have to go to work each day and finish specified assignments within a particular period of time. In many ways, this kind of work environment is easier to feel comfortable in than you may realize. One reason is that this involves institutional employment (working for a company) that involves an organizational structure and culture much like that of the educational institutions you have probably experienced already. Whether you like school or not, it is a familiar, stable, and relatively predictable institutional environment. In school, you know what you need to do and when you need to do it. It is understandable that some people would feel comfortable in a work environment with similar characteristics. Not only are those settings also relatively stable and predictable, but they provide employees with a paycheck as well. In such settings, good work habits are reinforced by the requirements and rewards of the job. As in school, your work environment will be relatively safe and secure.

For artists and free-lance designers, the situation is quite different. These individuals do not have a supervisor shaping their daily activities. This may sound like an attractive situation to you. If you didn't like the homework assignments you had to do in history class, then you may like the idea of not having a boss giving you creative assignments. In fact, it is true that for some people being on their own is the best thing for them. However, the situation is not quite as easy as it sounds. If you do not have a supervisor at work, you must be able to rely on yourself to set assignments and make sure that they are finished on time. You must also be responsible for quality control. No one will be standing over your shoulder telling you to try harder or do better. Moreover, you will be responsible for getting your own clients if you are a designer or selling your own work if you are an artist.

Perhaps the best way to say what is required of being on your own is that you must demand as much of yourself, in fact, more of yourself, than other people would demand of you. No one else will hold you accountable but yourself. In short, if you are on your own and want to be successful, you must learn to be self-disciplined and self-reliant.

TALENT

Perhaps by now you can guess why talent is not mentioned as the factor that contributes most to success in the field of art and design. The world is full of talented people who may have had promising futures but who never became artists because they were not truly committed to art, were not hard working, or lacked self-discipline. As in any professional field, success in art is driven by hard work and determination, perhaps more so than by any other factor. Before you consider the role of talent in an art career, you must understand that talent by itself is never enough to take you beyond the first few steps in achieving your career goals.

Having said that, however, it remains true that different people have different levels of artistic ability. Talented people generally do better than individuals with less talent. The question you may be asking yourself is, "Do I have enough talent to have a successful career in art or design?" Fortunately, you can get some fairly reliable help in answering that question. If you have done some art work already, you should show it to people who are in a position to give you an informed and unbiased assessment of your ability. These should not necessarily be people in your immediate family. Nor should they be your close friends. Friends and family members may not always give you the straightforward opinions you need. However, you should be able to find an art teacher—either a private art teacher, a high school art teacher, or someone who teaches art in a local college or university—who is willing to look at your work and discuss it with you. Because assessments of art can vary so much, it is a good idea to ask the opinions of more than one person. You also need to balance what they say against your own self-assessment and your own commitment to art.

CREATIVE INTELLIGENCE

It is commonly believed that there are two sides to art. That is reflected in the fact that we often experience art on an emotional level, but discuss it on an intellectual level. Because our emotional responses of liking or disliking certain art are so direct and immediate, the temptation is to assume that the making of art is fundamentally an emotional experience. In fact, for many artists it sometimes is. The emotional content of the art-making experience, however, should not distract us from understanding that creative intelligence is also required.

Intelligence comes in many forms. It is not exclusively related to the abstract reasoning that we associate with the study of mathematics or philosophy. Intelligence can also manifest itself in a full range of aesthetic capacities. Artists solve spatial problems and, therefore, must sometimes manipulate an enormously complex set of two- and three-dimensional visual elements. Art production requires a powerful mind that is capable of assessing the complexity of spatial terms.

Thus, artists must anticipate the quality of visual relationships before they are set down on paper, canvas, film, or stone. The problems of artistic synthesis are increased when the challenge of coordinating color, tone, and intensity is added to that of configuring spatial relationships. The mental ability of the artist is stretched yet again when formal issues such as line, form, mass, scale, depth, and color are used as the vehicle for expressing *ideas* through art. It is only through the disciplined application of creative intelligence that talent can be harnessed to produced good art.

SOURCES OF IDEAS AND INSPIRATION

Artists and designers do not produce work in a vacuum. They live and work in a world that is a constant source of ideas and inspiration.

Artists are particularly observant and therefore may often see things that other people do not. They find patterns, structures, objects, and colors that are visually interesting everywhere they look. Artists and designers are likely to see beauty in the patterns of shadows, the arrangement of cracks in the sidewalk, or the shape of old rusty tools casually discarded in a pile. The important point is that beauty is not an inherent quality of the shadows, sidewalk cracks, or rusty tools, rather it lies in the *perception* of artists. Their aesthetic perception is an important part of artistic creativity.

Artistic productivity, however, does not simply come about as result of creative potential. It comes about because artists are able to focus that potential on a particular artistic project. To put it in simple terms, artists have to draw, paint, sculpt, or photograph something. But what should that something be, and in what manner should that something be created? To answer this question, artists and designers need ideas. Creativity involves artistic ideas that are set down on paper or some other medium. Because ideas are so important to artists they often pay a great deal of attention to the world in which they live. Artists are usually well educated and well informed, and they often translate a variety of ideas directly into their art.

One important source of artistic ideas comes directly from the artist's personal experiences. Such factors as family background, personal ties, social circumstances, economic conditions, political ideals and religious beliefs, and emotional experiences may inspire the content of artistic production. Artistic inspiration sometimes develops out of an effort to reconcile and express the relationship between one's inner life and the reality of external conditions. It is this effort at reconciliation that makes art such an intensely personal experience.

Another source of ideas and inspiration is the work of other artists. Artists spend a lot of time looking at the cultural icons of their past. Great artists of the past may have worked on ideas that are the same as or similar to the concerns of contemporary artists and may therefore serve as a valuable reference or source of inspiration. For that reason, art history can play an important role as either a guide or point of departure for artistic production. Artists are also likely to be knowledgeable about the contemporary art scene for essentially the same kind of reason. In fact, sociologist Lawrence Shornack once described art production as a process in which artists sometimes work with the imaginary presence of particular artists looking over their shoulders with a critical eye.

LANGUAGE AND CONCEPT VISUALIZATION

Something important happened to the education of artists in the sixteenth and seventeenth centuries that changed the history of art. The training of artists in academics began to emphasize the acquisition of knowledge, including a familiarity with poetry, music, philosophy, history, and mathematics. There have been far reaching consequences as a result of this development and we will consider more of them when we look at art colleges and the education of artists. At this point, however, it is enough to understand the role of learning as a source of artistic ideas.

The written word brings images to life. This happens because language has the capacity to activate the mind; it is the medium through which concepts and concrete reality are visualized. The form of Japanese poetry called *haiku* is an excellent example of the relationship between language and visual imagery. These short seventeen-syllable poems have the power to evoke not only mental pictures but also the feelings and ideas that these images evoke. Here is an example of a seventeenth-century haiku by the great poet Basho.

> On a leafless bough
> In the gathering autumn dusk:
> A solitary crow!

But just as words can be used to represent visual images, so too can visual images be used to represent the ideas that words convey. This happens because images and ideas can stand for one another. This has critical implications in understanding the role of education in the careers of both fine and applied artists. It means that learning can be one of the most important sources of artistic ideas. Therefore, artists and individuals who wish to become artists should read as much as they can. Reading is an important way to develop a rich and lively artistic imagination.

Language and ideas have a deeper relationship. For the most part, artists can only produce images of things they can name. Language establishes categories of reality for the mind to contemplate and thus express in visual terms. Therefore, language does more than form a bridge between reality and image. In an important sense, language creates reality by sensitizing and informing perception. Artists are dependent on language as a means of increasing their ability to see creatively.

The relationship between images and ideas is, in many ways, the foundation for both fine and applied art. One of the several characteristics of fine art is its power to convey feelings or ideas that elevate or illuminate the human condition. This is why symbolism and the interpretation of art are considered to be so important. The applied arts—especially illustration, advertising design, and graphic design—are evaluated on a similar basis. The difference between the two kinds of art, however, is telling. The thoughts and feelings that fine art can evoke are often regarded as its ultimate objective. For the applied arts, by contrast, the ultimate objective is to elicit thoughts and feelings as a way to motivate particular kinds of behavior—especially consumer behavior.

DEVELOPING AN IDEA

A sociologist named Howard Becker once made an interesting distinction between art and craft. Art, he argued, is intended to produce unique or one-of-a-kind pieces of work. Craft, by contrast, has traditionally involved the development of virtuoso skills that enabled the craftsperson to make essentially the same thing over and over again in the same way—like making a matched set of coffee mugs or candle holders, for example. Printmaking and photography are interesting in this regard. They are both capable of producing multiple originals. These may be areas then where art and craft merge.

The idea that fine art always produces unique pieces of work is a bit misleading, however. Although it is true that the particular works of an artist may be unique as pieces of art, they may also be variations on a theme. Such an approach to art or design is sometimes referred to by artists as "developing" or "pushing" an idea. In the previous section, we saw that art and design are produced as a consequence of the aesthetic or artistic expression of an idea. A single artistic expression, however, does not exhaust all of the possibilities for the way in which the idea can be presented. Artists often try as many variations of an artistic idea as they can, especially if their artistic idea sells.

Some artists, such as Keith Haring, for example, seem to have a single artistic idea that is so commercially successful that they do not seem to change it in any significant way at all. In fact, you have probably seen the stick-figures on tee-shirts and in advertising that have made Haring so well known. Even such a great artist as Jackson Pollock repeated a similar artistic style which was commercially successful and therefore enabled him to sell his work. Sometimes the works are self-conscious efforts to develop the full range of possibilities for an artistic idea. These works are typically presented as a group of pieces called a "series."

There is an important point here for those who would like to become artists. Doing a single drawing or painting does not mean that you have learned all that you can learn from that one piece of work. If you have done something that you like or something that you think is interesting, try as many variations of it as you can until you have exhausted as many artistic possibilities as you can. Once you have explored an aesthetic idea fully, move on to new challenges so that your artistic ideas can continue to grow and develop.

EVOLVING AND EXPERIMENTING

One valuable consequence of developing an idea is that it enables you to move on to other ideas in a series of evolving stages. This happens as you begin to explore an artistic idea, develop the various possibilities that the idea has to offer, and then experiment with other ideas, building on what has come before. The work artists produce in that fashion involves not only the expression of artistic development, but also becomes a record of the evolution of their creative lives. Some artists radically change their artistic style and subject matter in a relatively abrupt way. The American artist Winslow Homer did so, for example, after traveling to the rugged Scottish coast. But the work of most artists moves progressively forward with each step along the way being a developmental consequence of the struggle to express ideas, explore them fully, and move on to new ideas.

The evolution of an artist's work may also be related to experimentation with technique and materials. Here, the challenges posed by an artist's medium may push his or her work in new directions. The desire for new artistic potential is one reason why artists work in mixed media. Mixed media or interdisciplinary approaches to art production are common and can often produce creative results.

THE CRAFTSMANSHIP OF ART

One part of the art-making process that is not always emphasized as much as it should be is the craft of art. The craft of art refers to the physical requirements of the processes and materials that are necessary to make art. This includes the technical aspects of art production that require practice and skill. There is an important hands-on quality to artistic production that many artists enjoy and acknowledge as essential to the art-making process. Aesthetic theory is interesting and valuable, but it can lose its significance if the artist cannot adequately manipulate the art medium.

Each medium will have a physical quality that is a source of satisfaction for the artist. Successful painters, sculptors, photographers, printmakers, illustrators, and graphic designers have all mastered the tools and materials of their trade. Even drawing—perhaps one should say especially drawing—has a directness and immediacy in the physical contact of pencil on paper that artists appreciate. Artists must be adept at using their tools and materials if they are to adequately bridge the gap between their artistic vision and what they put on paper.

COMPUTERS IN ART

A major new development in art is the use of computers. Computers allow an artist to produce two- and three-dimensional abstract and figurative works of art by "drawing" and "painting" with electronic lines, colors, and shapes on the computer screen. In addition, the computer will allow the artist to give the surface of rendered objects not only a seemingly limitless array of colors, but also a huge variety of textures, degrees of luster or shine, and various levels of brightness. It can also cast a shadow on the surface of an electronically rendered object that has been illuminated by an imaginary light source. This is especially important when computers are used to simulate real objects.

In some ways the computer is simply another kind of mechanism involved in art-making technology. The artwork produced by computers can have the same basic appearance as art produced with more familiar technology. An exhibit of fine art produced with computers will have a number of pieces that reveal an artistic imagination shaped by earlier use of conventional media. This is true for both abstract and figurative work. In addition, computer art is used in mixed media pieces.

Like any art technology, the use of computers is both liberating and confining for artists. The computer permits them to experiment in ways that seemed not to be previously available to the artist. It has always been possible, for example, to paint a picture that looks like computer art, yet before computers such images were generally not produced. Computer art sometimes has a distinctive look. Moreover, the textured surface qualities that make painting and sculpture so satisfying are not present in computer art, nor is the physical pleasure that some artists get from the craft of art making. Although computers can be intriguing and exciting, they remain only one among many artists' methods.

CHAPTER 3

ART AS A PROFESSION

The first chapter showed that even the most basic distinctions about art point to various ways in which it is practiced as a career, and the second chapter was intended to provide some insight into the creative process from which the arts emerge. However, people do not always think of art in this way. Art is more often thought about as a product— something to enjoy, think about, and discuss. We see the final product of art making in museums, art galleries, in department stores, in magazines, and even on television. But we do not often think of it in occupational terms, and we do not often think about how people actually make a living as artists.

The issue of earning a living through art is a serious one. It is therefore important to understand that art is a professional activity and that there are many kinds of careers in art. Art can be a struggle economically, especially in the early years of a career. It is also true, however, that an increasing number of people make a comfortable living by being artists, and in the remainder of this book we will explore the ways in which that is done. But it is also important to realize that in addition to being a means by which people can earn a living, art as an occupation can be rewarding in other ways.

The idea that art can be rewarding in a variety of ways is more important than it may initially appear to be. In addition to economic considerations, there are also psychological factors related to employment that are important because they have a direct impact on how you experience the work you do. These work-related psychological factors are sometimes referred to as job satisfaction. The reason that job satisfaction receives so much attention is that it contributes a great deal to the overall quality of a person's life. Remember that once you enter the world of work you may spend as many as 80,000 hours on the job. That is a great deal of time to spend doing something you do not enjoy. Ideally one would want to earn a living by doing something that is economically rewarding and enjoyable.

WHY ART IS A PROFESSION

Before we take an initial look at the various career areas in art, we should begin by understanding what kind of work art is. There are useful classifications for employment that are informative and can tell a lot about the nature of different kinds of work. Some of the well-known areas include blue-collar, clerical, and managerial occupations. Each broad job category has certain basic characteristics that tell us something about the fundamental and defining nature of an area of work. Art as a particular kind of occupation can be regarded as a "profession."

What is a profession? A profession is a category of work that has basic characteristics that make it distinct from other ways of earning a living. Those characteristics define not only the nature of work that professionals do, but also other important characteristics related to the occupation. Work may be characterized according to many factors. These factors include the length of training required as preparation for the profession; the theoretical as well as practical nature of that training; the development of it as a career, which increases in value over time; the freedom of practitioners from outside control over the practice of the profession; and the existence of associations that protect and promote the interest of the profession. There is, as well, something referred to as a "service ideology" which is the belief that the profession is of value or benefit to society. Occupations vary significantly in terms of the extent to which they are characterized by these features.

Art can be regarded as a profession because to one extent or another it involves each of these occupational characteristics. First, art involves long periods of training. While there may still be a few artists who may succeed without a college education, most artists have at least a bachelor of fine arts degree and many have the master of fine arts degree as well. This educational background takes several years of training. Beyond high school, formal art training may last four to six years. In addition, proficiency in art takes continued practice and development to reach one's full occupational potential. It is therefore similar to the length of training required of nurses, accountants, engineers, or public school teachers.

Second, art training requires learning more than skills and techniques. Today's artists must also be familiar with a wide range of ideas related to the important theoretical aspects of the visual arts. The interesting paradox in this is that art that is fundamentally conceptual can only be represented visually by the physical properties of the artist's material. Artists must learn not only the history and theory of art, but also a great deal of same kind of academic subject matter that forms the theoretical backbone of any program of undergraduate professional education. Traditional academic subjects such as literature, philosophy, and history can be a valuable source of artistic ideas.

Third, because art work involves individual creativity, artists must be left alone to produce their own ideas in environments that are conducive to creativity. Artistic creativity can only develop in situations that permit individuals to pursue their own ideas without intrusion or interference from others. This is why artists have valued their independence so much. Artists can be encouraged to work, but they cannot be forced to produce good art. Even graphic designers and illustrators who are employed by companies that produce work according to the specifications of clients must rely on their own creativity to translate those requirements into concrete ideas and images.

Fourth, there are several organizations and associations for applied arts areas and occupations, such as graphic design, interior design, art directors, publication designers, typographers, lithographers, and illustrators, that exist to promote the interests of the professionals they serve.

Together they specify guidelines for the assessment of educational programs, set standards for professional conduct, promote testing for technical competency, establish guidelines for contracts, and promote a variety of educational, advocacy, and professional service activities. The fine arts disciplines are not organized into associations that have the same kind of mandate. However, even here there are organizations and foundations that promote a variety of funding and support activities for the arts. Professional associations, organizations, and foundations for both the fine and applied arts can be found in the appendix B of this book.

Fifth, professions are distinguished from other occupations by the fact that they claim to provide services that are especially important to society. Fine art provides a number of important benefits: it can symbolize and thus express the most important values of a society, it can help establish and even promote useful patterns of cultural change, and it can serve as a basis for the development of a national cultural identity. The applied arts by definition produce concrete benefit to society. But in addition to promoting benefits of direct practical value, the applied arts can also make essentially the same kind of social and cultural contributions to society as the fine arts do. The social and cultural significance of art is important because it is assumed to be related to its market value.

Sixth, professions are characterized by the significant distinction between a job and a career. A job remains relatively static over time—it does not grow or change in a way that increases the occupational knowledge, skills, and value of the worker. A profession, by contrast, is characterized by occupational growth and development. Because an artist's occupational worth has the potential for continual expansion, art has the dynamic qualities of a career rather than the relatively static characteristics of a job. The developmental nature of a career can be reflected in an increase in the quality of an artist's work over time, and also in an increase in an artist's earning potential.

What is important to remember is that in addition to providing a means to earning a good living, art is satisfying for other reasons. People who want to become artists should understand the following about their profession: it requires long periods of training that involve both a technical and theoretical component, it requires artists to work independently without interference, it is organized into associations that promote the interests of members, it helps satisfy some of the basic needs of society, and it is characterized by the potential for ongoing occupational development. Many people consider these professional characteristics to be desirable and therefore regard art as a satisfying career choice.

TWO TRADITIONS IN ART

In the last chapter you learned that there are two basic theories of art. Art has been thought of as a means to express individual creativity or it has been thought of as satisfying some basic social needs. In reality, these two ideas are woven together. Art that is primarily expressive may also have some potential to satisfy practical social needs, and art that is primarily useful in its purpose will probably also be produced in a way that expresses the individual creativity of the artist. This is an important point because it says something fundamental about art as an occupation. The ideas that you should remember are that even when art is devoted purely to aesthetic objectives it can have a practical side, and that useful art can also seem to be produced with some concern for beauty.

When you consider art as a profession, you will see that it falls into two very broad categories. Art that is primarily concerned with individual creative expression and beauty is called fine art, and the art that is produced largely for practical reasons is typically referred to as applied art. All art is essentially divided along these lines. Each professional area occupies it own niche in the art world. The distinction between the fine and applied arts begins in art college and extends into a full range of areas, including the art market, art publications, and professional organizations. There are even professional jealousies between the two areas.

THE FINE ARTS

Earlier in this book, some of the kinds of media that are used to produce fine art were suggested. In fact, fine art is sometimes classified on the basis of such media as oil paint (painting), pencil (drawing), and stone (sculpture). There are additional media as well and these form the basis for the remaining classifications of fine art. These include film, printmaking, photography, and the electronic arts—such as video and computer art. Although each of these areas can constitute a world unto itself, there is a growing development in fine art toward what is called "mixed media," or art that is interdisciplinary in approach. Mixed media or interdisciplinary art combines material or techniques from more than one medium. The wall mounted works of Elizabeth Murray or Frank Stella seem to combine both painting and sculpture. Some of the photography of William Beckley contains as much drawing and written text as it does photographic images. Almost any of the art media you can think of have been combined with additional media to produce lively and imaginative works of art.

There are other ways in which fine art may be classified. One classification is based on the extent to which the work that is produced—whether it is drawing, sculpture, or photography—is either an abstract or a figurative representation of the real world. In a sense, all art is abstract because a representation of something is not the same as the thing itself. The job of the artist is to translate the "thing" into an image. But taken to its extreme, the distinction between abstract and representational art is based on the viewer's ability to recognize the work as something that one can see.

Today, this classification system is considered by some artists to be irrelevant to what it is their work is trying to achieve. They would argue instead that distinctions in art should be based on the content or meaning of their work. The content of art suggests another distinction based on what the work of art is about. Thus, art may represent the artist's emotional life, political convictions, or concerns for such formal aesthetic properties as line, composition, or color.

Other classifications may be based on the particular style that is common to artists who are producing work in roughly the same period of time. Thus, for example, art may be classified as being either abstract impressionism, cubism, or postmodernism. The influence of common cultural factors may have an impact on artists who have experienced their historical contexts in similar ways, thus producing a distinctive approach to art.

In sum, fine art may be classified in a variety of ways, depending on the purposes of the individuals who are doing the classifying. Fine art may be classified according to media (painting, printmaking, or video); it may be classified according to the aesthetic approach of the artist (abstract, representational, conceptual, or symbolic); or it may classified according to style (cubism, pointillism, or German expressionism). These are some of the more common classification systems but they are not the only ones. The reason that classification systems should be mentioned is because the various approaches to art suggested by these categories are very much tied to the economic realities of the art market. Anyone who makes a living in fine art will soon come to realize that the art market—the buying and selling of art—is to a large extent driven by changes in taste on the part of the art-buying public. This is just as true in the fields of applied art as it is in fine art.

THE APPLIED ARTS

The other basic approach to art as a profession is the applied arts. The applied arts have some kind of useful application and have therefore sometimes been called *commercial art*. As we have seen however, that term is not favored in the art world. The largest area in the applied arts is design. There are many kinds of design including advertising design, fashion design, graphic design, and interior design. There is even an art college in New York that offers a degree program in toy design. What these design areas have in common is a creative process that produces useful end results. Fashion design, for example, is used to create different styles of clothing; graphic design is used to create page layouts, book covers, company logos, as well as the designs that go on cereal boxes and other consumer packaging. Interior design is the basis for creating safe, comfortable, and aesthetically satisfying interior spaces in which people can live, work, and play.

There are other kinds of applied arts. Illustration is an especially important applied art. Illustration sometimes looks similar to representational fine art, and typically involves the use of drawings or paintings that are used to represent an idea, feeling, or message. Magazines often use illustrations to accompany stories or articles. Illustrations are also found in text books, children's books, brochures, catalogs, billboards, newspapers, product packaging, and advertising of all kinds. Cartooning is an interesting applied art and is sometimes considered to be a particular kind of illustration. Cartoons are used more widely than is sometimes realized. They appear in comic books, of course, but also in package design, political cartoons, advertising, and in public service messages.

Photography is a medium that is used to produce both fine and applied art. The applied art applications of photography are perhaps the most pervasive and widely recognized. Applied photography is used in books, magazines, newspapers, brochures and catalogs, on billboards, and in political campaigns. It is especially important in print advertising of all kinds. Advertisers are well aware of the familiar aphorism that a picture is worth a thousand words. However, when pictures are combined with words the result can produce an even more compelling effect.

Two other important applied art areas focus on the significance of art making as a process rather than the products of art production. These areas are art education and art therapy. Art education involves the teaching of art in kindergarten through the twelfth grade. In most public school systems, and in private schools as well, art is considered an important part of the education young people receive. It is thought to promote their creative and imaginative abilities and introduce them to a basic hands-on art appreciation experience. The individuals who teach art to young people have made art education a career. You may already have had contact with such a person either in grammar school or high school.

The other applied art area that focuses on process more than product is art therapy. This field is based on the expectation that individuals with a variety of physical and/or emotional problems can benefit from the personally enriching process of creating art. It is assumed, for example, that art can enable individuals to express feelings that would otherwise be blocked. This is true for people of any age. Art therapy is a growing field and practitioners work in a variety of settings, but are most often found in psychiatric, general, and Veterans Administration hospitals.

WEARING TWO HATS

In some areas in art—such as art education or art therapy, interior design, or graphic design—people work for a company as an employee. These individuals are like other people in the labor market in that they work for one employer at a time doing a basic type of work or a range of related kinds of tasks. These individuals may work for a school, publishing company, advertising firm, or a graphic design or interior design company. Their work is creative and unique, but in some important respects they share many of the basic employment characteristics of people who are nurses, sell insurance, or work in a bank. I will speak more about these employment characteristics in subsequent chapters. At this point, however, I want to speak about those individuals who do not work for a company.

A variety of individuals work for themselves as artists or designers. Fine artists, of course, are really very much like independent businesspeople. They produce their own artworks and sell them in galleries. They may also receive funding through government grants for artists. Some designers also work for themselves. In fact, almost anyone who does photography or illustration does so on a free-lance basis, and many people who work in fashion design or interior design do so as well. Working "free-lance" means being on your own and selling your art or design work to clients who are willing to pay for your service.

Working on a free-lance basis is a double-edged sword. It is ideal for individuals who want to be on their own and who can handle the rewards and responsibilities of working independently. It can also be a source of frustration during those times when business is slow and clients are scarce. Until you reach a point in your free-lance work where you have built up a sufficient client list so that you can maintain some cash flow even in periods of economic downturn, you may very well experience times when you will need to look for alternate sources of income.

These alternate sources of income may be just as satisfying as the art or design work itself. Many artists and designers work at any number of interesting and well-paying jobs. Individuals may work in positions such as gallery directors, art teachers, or account executives for design firms. But it may also mean that in the very early stages of your career, you may have to work at jobs that do not have a great deal of glamour or earning potential until you find your niche in the art world. If this sounds a bit familiar to you, it may be because actors and musicians sometimes face similar employment patterns that allow them to earn a living while they develop their art. This means that you may need to be prepared to wear two hats during the early part of your career. One will enable you to pay the rent; the other will allow you to produce your art.

A CAREER IN ART

Art as a career is unlike most other professions, and it is advisable to have a clear sense of what makes it so distinctive. Art is something that creative individuals feel compelled to do. This may not be easy to understand for people who are of a purely pragmatic bent of mind. From their points of view, earning a living is the primary means by which to pursue life's goals. For such individuals, the means of achieving this objective are often secondary.

For artists, it is a different matter because their primary motivation is the creative process and the desire to produce art. Yet creative self-actualization doesn't have much meaning without a concern for economic reality. Thus, artists need to be as concerned with the practical issues related to career as they are with issues of self-expression. These are not simply idle contemplations. They call attention to the need to lead a creative yet balanced and productive professional life. We will now turn to the basic issues of employment in the fine and applied arts.

CHAPTER 4

FINE ART AS AN OCCUPATION

Drawing, painting, sculpture, printmaking, and photography are the five primary kinds of fine art. They are represented in art museums and galleries more often than other media. However, interesting and exciting work is also produced through computer art, video, ceramics, glass making, and fiber art. Artists will often become involved in several of these media at various points in their careers, and may also move back and forth between them. It is also true that artists will sometimes combine media to such an extent that it is not always easy to classify a work of art according to materials of production.

Artists who work in the various fine arts disciplines have a great deal in common from an occupational point of view. One distinguishing characteristic of fine artists is that they work alone. Most other professionals—doctors, lawyers, or teachers are examples—are engaged in work that involves interaction with specific clients or segments of the population. In addition, most of these professionals work in institutional settings, involving ongoing relationships with a wide range of colleagues and staff. Fine artists, by contrast, generally work without much assistance, advice, or consultation from anyone.

Perhaps the most central fact of economic life for fine artists is that they produce work for which there is no specific ready-made market. The basic problem for all artists is getting their art into the art market and having it accepted by the buying public. Actually, these two economic issues are very much interrelated.

THE GALLERY SYSTEM

An art gallery is essentially a boutique or specialty store in which art is sold. Depending on the size of the art work and amount of available space, a gallery may have as few as ten and up to as many as two hundred pieces of art or more. Galleries are where artists exhibit and sell their artwork. Galleries lie at the heart of the art market.

Artists usually begin to exhibit or show their work while they are in art college. Shows that take place in school give students the experience of presenting work to a public audience and it also begins to establish their résumé. Graduate school can give students additional opportunities for gallery exposure. Other possibilities for exposure include art competitions, as well as city or regional art programs that bring art to the public. Competitions enable students to submit their work and have it evaluated by a jury. These competitions may lead to honors, cash prizes, or exhibitions.

In order to sell art, however, an artist must be able to find a gallery that is willing to show it. But to have a show of an artist's work, a gallery must know that it exists. There are some galleries that are willing to look at the photographic slides of an artist's work. This is perhaps the least efficient way to have your work taken seriously by a gallery dealer and accepted for a show, especially in a large city like New York. In large cities, there are many artists who are available and dealers can therefore be selective. In smaller cities where there may be fewer good artists, a dealer is much more likely to accept an artist based on looking at slides and portfolios.

It is also possible to reach the art-buying public through artists' cooperatives. These are galleries run by artists who pay money to rent space and show their work. This set-up enables artists to pay for gallery exposure until they are able to establish contact with a dealer who is willing to accept their work. The exposure is valuable, but cooperatives usually take a lot of time and energy because, in addition to paying rent, artists have administrative chores to attend to, such as maintaining the gallery space, scheduling shows, and staffing the facility. Also, showing in a cooperative gallery is often based more on financial resources than artistic ability. Cooperative galleries tend to exist at the lower end of a gallery hierarchy that is highly stratified.

More typically, an artist will be introduced to a dealer through another artist or someone else connected to the gallery. The process of "networking," or getting to know people who have contacts in the art world, is therefore very important. Artists who are have nearly completed art college or have recently graduated may be introduced to dealers by their art teachers. This is one of several reasons why it is important to attend an art college with faculty who are themselves active professional artists. Students can begin to make important professional contacts through faculty while in undergraduate as well as graduate degree programs. These contacts can prove to be invaluable.

A gallery will either select one or two pieces of an artist's work as part of a group show, or it may have a solo exhibition featuring the work of a single artist. Both kinds of exhibits are important because they enable an artist's work to be seen by the buying public. Any exposure is valuable. Generally speaking, however, a solo show carries with it more prestige for the artist and is therefore a better vehicle for selling work and developing a reputation. There are some group shows, however, that are extremely important in terms of their impact on an artist's reputation. The Whitney Museum Biennial would be an example. This is where the issue of getting a gallery show and having work accepted by the public begin to converge.

Having work shown in a gallery does two critically important things simultaneously. It exposes the artist's work to the consuming public, and it validates the worth of the work in the eyes of prospective buyers. The issue from a marketing point of view is that gallery exposure can influence the perceptions of people who see the work.

It is obvious that having work accepted by a gallery is an important part of developing one's career as an artist. There is another issue to consider, however. It is also important to have one's work accepted by the right kind of gallery. A major concern is getting work into the best gallery possible. An artist's work is judged, in part, by the quality of the gallery in which it appears. Galleries are hierarchically ranked in terms of reputation and prestige. Galleries with good reputations will increase the value of the art they show. Conversely, galleries with poor reputations will call the value of the art they show into question. It is important to have one's first few shows in a good gallery. That will set the stage for subsequent evaluations by dealers who will want to know where the artist's work has been shown.

Another concern is finding a gallery whose dealer has compatible aesthetic sensibilities. This is less of a concern in smaller cities, where galleries tend to generalize and will exhibit an eclectic array of work. Galleries in larger cities, on the other hand, tend to specialize in particular kinds of art. Artists ideally like to show work in galleries that have a solid reputation, and are known for promoting work they find compatible to their own. The key is to establish visibility in a credible and compatible gallery context.

Galleries sell art work for a commission and will typically take 50 percent of the price of the work they sell. Artists and dealers have a highly interdependent yet sometimes strained relationship. They cannot do without each other, yet each may feel as though his or her contribution has greater value in the relationship. Because of the potential for problems that artists may face in dealing with galleries, it is important that an artist find a dealer with whom a comfortable relationship can be established. Avoiding personality conflicts can go a long way toward resolving problems before they occur.

The best way for an artist to avoid problems, however, is to conduct relationships with gallery dealers on strictly business terms. This means signed contracts between the artists and dealers. There are a variety of contracts covering different kinds of professional relationships with galleries. These arrangements include consignment agreements, exclusive contracts, and monthly allowances against total sales. An understanding must be reached on a number of matters, such as when payment for sales will be made, who absorbs courtesy discounts for large purchases, and any out-of-gallery sales. Two useful guides to handling the business side of art are *The Business of Art* (2nd ed.) by Lee Caplin and *The Business of Art: A Comprehensive Guide to Business Practices for Artists* by Diane Cochrane.

There is one other matter that can be of concern to artists. Because there is a relationship between the artistic product and the marketability of the work, some dealers are inclined to make suggestions about such creative matters as the size, materials, or content of an artist's work. Artists vary in their response to that kind of input. Those who place particular emphasis on selling their work may be receptive to suggestions from dealers who know what sells. Other artists let such suggestions go in one ear and out the other. In either case, the primary responsibility of the artist in relationship to gallery dealers will be the quality control of artistic production.

SPECIALIZED GALLERIES

Galleries can specialize in a number of ways. The work they sell can be from a particular historical period, or, in the case of contemporary art, they can represent the artistic taste or vision of the dealers. But galleries can also specialize in the medium used to create the work. Some galleries, for example, may specialize in photography or sculpture. Specialization gives galleries a distinctive position in the art market.

Other galleries specialize in work that has traditionally been recognized as craft. The term *craft* refers to work that is primarily defined by utilitarian or practical purpose. These works are created using traditional methods and materials. Typical examples of craft works include useful objects made of ceramics, glass, and fiber. In recent years those methods and materials have been used to create works that are not primarily utilitarian in value. These works are singular in design, are created for the same expressive and aesthetic reasons as paintings or sculpture, and may cost may thousands of dollars. In such cases, craft work should really be regarded as art.

It may not always be easy, however, to tell when a piece of work is art or craft. Consider a glass vase that is made by hand and costs $500. If it was made to be used as a vase, then its usefulness may define it as craft work. But what about a unique handmade vase that costs $12,000 and is displayed as a piece of sculpture in an executive office, museum, or other public space? That kind of example would be defined by its aesthetic value rather than by its potential practical value. Second, if people were to think of it as a piece of "art," then by that definition it would have to be regarded as art. As discussed in Chapter 1, if this question is viewed from a sociological point of view, then art is whatever people and institutions in society define it as being. The more difficult examples to define would be those works that are an ambiguous mix of practicality and beauty.

Just as there is a hierarchy of galleries for traditional art, there is a hierarchy for ceramics, glass, and fiber as well. There are relatively few galleries in the United States that specialize only in the highest quality work in these media, but recognition of such work is growing. There are many more outlets for work that sells at a more modest price. Some of these outlets include gift shops, furniture stores, accessory shops, and annual craft fairs. Works at the lower end of the price scale are much more likely to be regarded as craft in the traditional sense of the term.

ART MUSEUMS

Galleries generally sell the work of artists but do not collect it. Museums, by contrast, will buy the work of artists and keep it in their collections. A museum will acquire the work of an artist in one of three ways. First, the museum curator may hear about an up-and-coming artist through insiders who are close to the art scene—perhaps the artist has gotten good press as the result of a solo show. The curator may then buy one of the artist's works directly from the gallery and add it to the museum's collection. Second, a curator may go out and look for new artists or for artists who are doing a particular kind of work that the museum may want to have. The curator will then comb the galleries to find new work to buy. Third, an art collector may donate a piece of work to a museum to help enhance an artist's reputation or as a tax deductible contribution. In either case, a museum will take only the best of what is offered. The artist's work will first be evaluated and then accepted by a museum, which will want to take every precaution to maintain its reputation.

Having one's work accepted by a museum is a major step in an artist's career. There are many artists but only a relatively few of them have their works in the collections of museums. Just as there is a hierarchy among galleries, there is also a hierarchy among museums. In the United States, the most important museums are usually in major cities, but many small cities have fine museums as well.

The significance of having one's work in a museum collection will depend in part on the reputation of the museum. The significance of the reputation of the museum or gallery, however, needs to be assessed in the context of two economic systems. First, all work will be judged in terms of where it stands in relationship to the national and international art scene. Second, art is also judged in terms of where it stands within a particular art market. The purpose of an evaluation will determine the context for comparison.

Thus, the status and the marketability of art by a local artist whose work has been accepted by a museum in a small city may not stack up very well when it is compared to the status and marketability of art by an internationally known artist whose works are in major museums in New York or Paris. Yet the more important point is that works of art find their own market levels and can contribute to the economic success and prestige of artists in a local as well as in an international context.

Museums and their effects on the value of art may seem a long way off for young artists who are at the beginning of their careers. Yet, successful artists are often discovered by important galleries and museums at relatively early ages. Artists in their twenties and thirties who have made it to the big time are common. It is also true, however, that very young people do not achieve artistic recognition, as they do in classical music. Most artists must at least get through undergraduate if not graduate art college before gaining prominence.

ART CONSULTANTS

Museums are not the only institutions to buy art. Art is also purchased by large and small businesses. Small businesses need art for lobbies, reception areas, and offices. The art for small companies is likely to be bought by the company owner or an employee of the company. If a company moves into a new space that is being renovated, an interior designer may acquire art for the new offices. An art purchase such as this is likely to be made by someone who is not a specialist in art.

There are consultants, however, who specialize in purchasing art for companies. These individuals typically work for major corporations with large budgets for art. The consultants help the individuals or art selection committees in corporations who are responsible for purchasing art. Corporations purchase art for a variety of reasons. They may want to place art in executive offices, meeting rooms, reception areas, and lobby spaces of company headquarters. Or a company may want to purchase art as a means of showing visible support for the arts. Some companies, such as hotels and restaurant chains, may need art as part of the interior design for areas used by customers.

Art consultants sometimes work as staff members of large interior design and architectural firms. These firms often provide a wide range of services to clients who need new or renovated office spaces. A company that hires an architect to build a new headquarters or regional office may ask for help in purchasing art. A large architectural firm may have an in-house art consultant who can provide that service.

There are two basic approaches to purchasing art for corporations: art is either purchased primarily for its decorative value, or it is purchased with a concern for its enduring artistic qualities. Art of the first kind is typically used to accent customer contact areas in restaurants, movie theaters, or hotels. Such art is typically not expensive, and must be purchased with a concern for decorative issues such as color, size, and subject matter. Art of the second kind is typically purchased with a concern for investment value. The credentials and reputation of the artist are much more important for this kind of purchase. This is where the knowledge and expertise of the art consultant becomes most useful.

When a company wants to build or add to its corporate art collection, it will hire a consultant who will be paid directly by the firm for services rendered. Such a contact is an important aspect of the art consulting business. How it should be handled has been clearly spelled out in the guidelines of the Association of Corporate Art Consultants as well as by the Association of Professional Art Advisors. Consultants should not receive a percentage of the sale from the corporation, the artist, or the gallery from whom the art work is bought. This guideline helps prevent the conflict of interest that might develop if a consultant's fee were to be tied to the dollar value of the sale.

An art consultant who has been hired to purchase valuable art will have a slide library of the work of many artists. The consultant will show slides of several artists whose work might satisfy the client's requirements. Once the client selects a few possibilities, the consultant may show the actual artwork. When the final selections have been made, the purchase takes place through the consultant. The consultant will purchase the artwork on behalf of the client through a gallery that represents the artist, or will purchase the art directly from the artist if that individual markets work without using a gallery.

It is worth noting that corporate collections play a significant role in the art world. Most important, perhaps, is that their purchases of art provide a significant source of income for artists. In addition to that, however, corporate art collections serve to legitimate the art they hold. It is assumed that work held in the collections of important corporations such as IBM and others has significant aesthetic and market value. Given the knowledge and expertise of art consultants who help shape corporate collections, that assumption is often justified. It is therefore not surprising that corporate collections are often known for their quality. For that reason, artists' résumés will prominently display the names of corporate collections that have purchased their work.

PRIVATE COLLECTORS

Private collectors play a major role in the art world. Focused collections can consolidate and preserve disparate works of art that might not be brought together in any other way. They can also stimulate the development of the art they support through their patronage. Collectors will purchase and hold works of art and then they will either display or keep them in storage. Because collectors have buying power, they can be of direct economic value to artists. Collectors can also have a great deal of impact on the art market. The more work of a particular artist they buy, the greater will be the perceived value of that artist.

The buying patterns of collectors typically fall into one of four categories. First, some collectors will purchase a single work of an artist simply because of the artist's reputation. Such collectors will want to have work by a "hot" new artist in their collection. From the point of view of artists, such collectors seem to acquire art in an impromptu and rather meaningless way. These one-time collectors are a momentary event in the economic life of an artist. There are some impromptu collectors who will purchase more than one work by a particular artist. These collectors can be more important to an artist because they buy more work.

Second, there are collectors who want to build collections that are focused in particular ways. Each will acquire the work of an artist because it makes a contribution to the theme of his or her particular collection. These collectors can add status as well as income to artists because of the care, intelligence, and discrimination that they use to build their collections.

The third kind of collector also builds collections, but rather than acquiring work of a period or based on another theme, this individual will collect the work of a particular artist. This is perhaps the most important kind of collector, at least from the point of view of the fortunate artist whose work is being purchased. Such collectors make ongoing commitments to the long-range value of the artists whose works they purchase. Such relationships between artists and collectors may take on a personal as well as economic dimension. In such cases, they will sometimes know one another personally and spend time with one another socially.

THE ECONOMIC ROLE OF CRITICS

An art critic can influence the public's perception of the value of an artist's work, just as a movie critic can influence the public's perception of the worth of a movie. The important difference, however, is that in the case of a movie, people usually like what they like despite the comments of a critic. The same is not quite true in the world of art. For one thing, one's own taste is not the only factor to consider in an art purchase. It might be if one were purchasing a single painting to go over the fireplace or behind the sofa. But that is not the case for people who are serious collectors. For these people, art is something to be enjoyed but also something that has economic value that will either grow or diminish. These people want to have confidence that the art they buy will increase or at least maintain its value. Moreover, there are some collectors who purchase art exclusively as an investment. These people will turn to art critics for an opinion, especially when a painting or piece of sculpture costs many thousands of dollars.

Critics publish their opinions in magazines, newspapers, and special art journals. Critics in newspapers like the *New York Times* in the United States or *Le Figaro* in Paris publish opinions that carry much weight. Art journals such as *Art in America, Art Forum, Arts Magazine, Art News,* and *Art Papers* publish reviews that can be very important to an artist. These journal reviews focus on work that is currently showing in galleries. A strong review by a critic can add much to the reputation and therefore economic value of an artist's work. The New York artist William Beckley has speculated that one strong review in an important art journal may be worth as many as six or seven gallery exhibitions toward enhancing an artist's reputation.

ART STYLES AND THE ART MARKET

Some artists establish such strong reputations that the economic value of their work will transcend the vagaries of the art market. These are usually deceased artists who are of such historical significance that their work will retain its value no matter what the current art trends happen to be. For living artists, however, the economic value of art they sell will be determined, at least in part, by its significance within the context of an art market that is responsive to changing fashion and taste. In this way, the art market is subject to some of the same kinds of forces that affect the value of other commodities over time.

As trends in art change, the market value of certain styles or artists will also change. There are artists who are very much in the center of things for a period of time and then seem to fade from the scene. What is considered to be important art during one period of time may become less popular later. This does not mean that art is as disposable as bell-bottom pants or yesterday's hair style, but it does mean that the career of an artist over time may need to be responsive to the realities of changes in the art market.

One force that can sometimes suppress artistic change is success. Artists who are able to sell their work may be reluctant to substantially alter what they produce. It is also true that gallery dealers thrive on consistency and are therefore leery about seeing their best artists move into new and uncharted territories. These factors can inhibit an artist's ability to move with or anticipate changing art currents.

In Chapter 2, we saw that artists will develop ideas until they are satisfied that they have explored as many aesthetic possibilities with them as they can. That desire for exploration and experimentation will push artists into new directions. This is an important driving force behind creativity, but it is not the only one. The realities of an ever-changing art market also have the potential to influence the work of an artist. Few artists are indifferent to what sells and what does not. Such observations can have an impact on what artists perceive to be aesthetically satisfying in their own work. Not all artists are moved by such forces, but the potential for such influence is real. For sincere artists who want to sell their work, the challenge may be to balance artistic integrity with the economic reality of the public taste in art.

THE MARKET VALUE OF ART

There are essentially two approaches to the question of the value of art. One focuses on philosophical questions related to the relationship between art and human experience. From this point of view, the value of art is judged in terms of aesthetic qualities and their impact on people. Thus, art is judged to be valuable if it satisfies our need for aesthetic experience, gives us insight into the human condition, or promotes the cultural life of society. From an economic point of view, however, the value of art is determined by what people are willing to pay for it. It is typically assumed, or at least hoped, that there is a positive relationship between the aesthetic quality of art and its price. Yet a basic question remains—how is the price determined?

Prices for art are set by the gallery dealer and artist together. The price is arbitrary yet determined by a variety of factors. One of those factors is the subjective evaluation that the dealer and artist make of the quality of the art. This kind of judgment is based on experience and knowledge of the quality of other art, the price of which has been established.

Somewhat more objective factors that are also taken into account include the number and the importance of gallery shows the artist has had, the amount of money the artist's work has sold for in the past, and the number and quality of reviews of the artist's work. This last factor is especially important. In addition, the size of the artwork can be a factor. Larger pieces generally sell for a higher price than smaller pieces by the same artist. All of this means that the price of art is determined by subjective perceptions and objective market factors.

Another significant consideration is the general economic climate during which art is sold, as well as the particular economic condition of the art market itself. During the 1980s, for example, art was considered to be a good economic investment. A lot of art was bought during that period of time with the realistic expectation that its value would continue to rise. The value of art did rise, but it rose beyond what the market could sustain. When people who bought at high prices tried to sell, they could not always do so. When buyers realized that the market was overinflated, they stayed away from the market or only bought work that had a more traditional appeal.

Young artists who anticipate the prospect of selling their first works sometimes have unrealistically high expectations. An artist who has not previously had a gallery show and whose work is not known in the art community may have difficulty selling work for more than a few hundred to a few thousand dollars, depending on the prestige of the gallery and size of the city where the work is being sold. The value of an artist's work, however, will increase gradually and often dramatically over time.

EDUCATIONAL CREDENTIALS

The résumé has become an increasingly important part of the artist's marketing strategy. By producing and showing good work, artists build a strong résumé. The importance of a résumé is that gallery dealers and private collectors want to feel assured about the quality of an artist's work. Assessing the quality of art work, however, is not always easy to do because the evaluation criteria are not necessarily easy to define and because the evaluation process is partly based on opinion. That is why the number of gallery shows, reviews, and museum holdings are important. Although they are also based on subjective perceptions, they at least provide independent evidence that other individuals and institutions in the art world have acknowledged the significance of the artist's work.

Something else that can help to validate the subjective opinions of art is the educational background of the artist. A strong educational background allows the inference that an artist's work has developed out of a specific institutional tradition of knowledge, expertise, and artistic success. That is why the quality of the art college and type of degree can play a role in perception of an artist's work. The substance of an artwork is expected to be associated with educational credentials of the artist.

GRANTS AND OTHER FUNDING SOURCES

Young artists as well as more established artists receive support from government sources. The National Endowment for the Arts (NEA) is a major funding source. It supports such organizations as the Southern Arts Federation and the many other arts programs and institutions around the country that award grants to artists. Cities as well as state councils and commissions on the arts also make grants to artists. There are a number of publications that provide information about the grants and other sources of support for artists. Some of these include *Art & Culture Funding Report, The Washington International Arts Letter, Money to Work: Grants for Visual Artists,* and *Money for Visual Artists* by Suzanne Niemeyer. Magazines such as *Art Week* and *Afterimage* also list funding sources for individual artists. Another useful source for announcements of juried art shows is a periodical called *Art Calendar.* A good source for information on a variety of resources including workshops, seminars, conferences, internships, fellowships, assistant- ships, scholarships, artists-in-residence programs, arts councils, and art competitions is the *National Arts Placement Newsletter.*

In addition to providing needed funding to help support an artist's work, these grants and competition awards can also reaffirm an individual's feelings of self-worth as an artist. In a practical sense, the artist actually becomes more valuable from a marketing point of view by increasing his or her reputation which, in turn, influences other people's perception of the art.

Another valuable resource that can provide information and referral to organizations is the Visual Artists Information Hotline (1-800-232-2789). The hotline provides information on funding, insurance, legal assistance, artist colonies and residences, public art programs, and other services for artists. Visual artists can use the hotline to make a free call from anywhere in the U.S. and reach the Arts Resource Consortium Library in New York City. The service is available Monday through Friday from 2:00 P.M. to 5:00 P.M. Eastern Standard Time.

ALTERNATIVE SOURCES OF INCOME

It is important to realize that only some fine artists make a living exclusively from the sale of their artworks. This is especially true at the early stages of their careers. For that reason one must begin to anticipate the prospect of finding alternative sources of income. This situation may or may not be discomforting to a young artist. Many alternative sources of income are a satisfying part of a flexible professional career. College teaching is one of the most important and satisfying ways that an artist can find to support a budding art career.

One source of occupational flexibility for fine artists is especially appealing. It involves working in both the fine and applied art areas. Painters, for example, may do illustration or photography. Fine art photographers may do free-lance work as applied art photographers. Fine artists may also have a background in graphic design and may work in that capacity as well. There are many career-enhancing possibilities for imaginative and entrepreneurial artists. An open mind and resourceful attitude will be valuable for any artist who seeks to take advantage of available opportunities.

CHAPTER 5

APPLIED ART AS A CAREER I: WORKING FOR A COMPANY

Design companies are really human service organizations. They produce a finished product but their real function is to help clients resolve a problem or satisfy a need. This places a full range of demands on the artist's technical, personal, and communication skills. Artists and designers must be able to understand what the client needs and convey ideas about how those needs can be addressed through particular design solutions. In addition, people who are employed by design companies and design departments within large corporations must be able to work in a team. Each member of the team contributes his or her special skill, knowledge, and expertise to the design project as it develops over time. This system also places demands on the designer's ability to work effectively with people in an institutional context.

Some artists and designers may not feel comfortable working in these complex social environments. Such individuals may find the relative independence of free-lance work more appealing. Nonetheless, even the most individualistic and free-spirited person will probably need to spend at least some time working in an organizational setting. There are two reasons for this. First, until an individual has built a portfolio of professional work that demonstrates his or her ability, getting free-lance work will not be easy. Second, even though art schools do an excellent job preparing students to enter the world of work, they cannot teach them all of the important tricks of the trade that come from years of experience. Working for a design firm for at least a few years can place the young artist or designer in the company of seasoned professionals who can provide valuable on-the-job training.

This chapter will cover four basic areas of art and design: graphic design, advertising design, interior design, and fashion design. These applied arts areas cover a wide range of occupational experiences that can be extrapolated to other career areas.

GRAPHIC DESIGN

Graphic design is a term that covers a variety of specializations, such as book design, magazine design, logo design, package design, and typography. Unlike illustration or fine art areas such as painting in which artists work by themselves on a project, graphic design involves a number of different individuals whose creative talents and activities are integrated into a common team effort.

Graphic designers may be called on to design page layouts for a magazine, a company logo, a system of informational signs for the interior of an organization (environmental design), a brochure, a shopping bag, banners, labels for consumer products, trade show graphics and displays, cassette or compact disc covers, the menu for a restaurant, a company's annual report, or packaging for a new product. A major task of graphic designers is to design the layout of the printed page. This involves organizing the text or copy, selecting the lettering, and arranging any photographs or illustrations on a page. Page layout is done for magazines, books, brochures, newsletters, and pamphlets.

The Design Process

Whatever the specific job may be, the first phase of any design project begins with the client. A meeting will be set up to discuss exactly what kind of services the client needs. In one way or another, the client will want the designer to call attention to either a product or a service, or to organize information or other printed matter.

How the designer does that will depend on a variety of factors that must be taken into account. The designer must be aware of such things as the demographic characteristics of the customers or users of their clients' services, the tastes or preferences of those customers, the design approach of the clients' competitors, and the specific style trends related to colors, images, shapes, and so forth. Experienced designers may already be familiar with some of this important background information. It is also likely, however, that research will be required.

After discussions with the client, the designer should have clear idea of what the client needs. A series of meetings will then take place at the design studio to determine what kind of talents and skills are needed on the design team for the particular job. In addition to one or more graphic designers, for example, the team may require a photographer, a writer to prepare the copy if that is required, and a typographer to style lettering.

The initial round of meetings will focus primarily on developing basic ideas. The designer may do a number of preliminary sketches to work out some basic design ideas on paper. The creative director on the team will then take the best design ideas and have them developed into somewhat more detailed drawings called "comps" ("comprehensive" representations of the basic design ideas). The drawings will go through a series of stages, including "thumb-nail comps," "marker comps," and "finished comps."

When the designer is satisfied with the ideas that have been developed, a finished or presentation comp is prepared and shown to the client for approval. At some point along the way, the client will feel satisfied with the design and the process will move forward to production. At this point, the designer becomes responsible for not only the basic design, but also for the budget—which is often discussed early in the process—and schedule, as well as the production specifications of the project. If a pamphlet or brochure is being designed, the designer will take bids and hire a printer. The designer will also have to select the color and weight of the paper and the color of the ink used in printing. All of this is done with a series of predetermined deadlines.

The final phase of the design process happens when the "mechanicals" (these consist of written copy, art work, and type positioned and mounted on a board for photomechanical reproduction) are prepared and sent to the printer. At this point, "brown line" or "blue line" contact prints are made from photographic negatives of the mechanicals and are checked for any errors. This is a critical step because the public will see the final product, and errors can be embarrassing and costly for all concerned. The design work is then ready for printing.

The Organization of Design

There is as much variation in the basic staff makeup of design companies as there is in the various phases of the design process. There are three basic things to know about design organizations. First, much design work will either be done in design firms or in the design departments of large corporations. Design firms only do design. They provide design work for other companies that require their services.

The work done by design companies tends to focus on the need that a client company has to communicate with its customers or clients. Some work of this nature can be perceived as being relatively glamorous. This is especially true when the design work increases the client's ability to earn income, has a high level of visual appeal, and has the potential to reach a large audience. Such results can significantly enhance the reputation of the designer. This is especially true for any work that is associated with package design for products that are widely known or for other kinds of national campaigns. Designers often gain prestige and recognition from client companies that have a high degree of visibility or that are well known.

By contrast, much of the work that is done by the design department of a large corporation is focused on in-house needs. Internal publications—newsletters, training manuals, or corporate reports—tend to be handled by the in-house design department. In addition, the corporate design department will typically handle new applications for existing designs. For example, this responsibility might entail making use of an existing design that is used on packaging for a new company product, or it might entail making some modifications of an established package design. In either case, the designer will be responsible for working with an established design rather than creating and developing a new design concept. When the company reaches a point where it needs to embark on a major design overhaul of its packaging or company logo, an outside design firm is often brought in to handle this specialized assignment.

This means that work done by an in-house design department is not always the most creative or glamourous, but the pay and benefits for starting designers are good. An individual may expect to start at $18,000 to $22,000 plus benefits, such as health insurance and vacations. The salary will vary depending on size of the city as well as region of the country where the firm is located. Another benefit of starting one's career in a design department is that large corporate budgets often permit departments to purchase the best available material and equipment. Working with state-of-the-art professional equipment can be a valuable experience for a young designer. Moreover, working for a large corporation with a high degree of visibility or name recognition can enable a designer to strengthen his or her résumé and portfolio.

Second, design companies will either specialize in a particular kind of design work, or will provide a more general range of design services. To some extent this will depend on the size of the city in which the design company is located. In New York, where there is a flourishing market for design, it is possible for a company to specialize in two-dimensional or "flat" design work. This work involves the kind of graphic design that one might find in magazines or with compact discs. Or it may be possible for a company to specialize in three-dimensional work, such as package design or exhibition design. In New York as well as in smaller cities, many companies are likely to do a variety of kinds of design. Especially in a slow economic period, few companies will be in a position to turn work away. Therefore, students in art school would be well advised to get as broad a design education as they can in order to increase their versatility and thus their attractiveness to prospective employers.

There can be advantages to working in either kind of design firm. On the one hand, specialized firms can give designers valuable expertise in a design area for which there is proven demand. On the other hand, the design generalist will have a more flexible range of skills and knowledge to offer a prospective employer. In the final analysis, a young designer's future may be more the result of luck in finding a job than it is in rational planning and early efforts at career management.

There are other institutional settings in which design work is done, however. These include department stores, newspapers, television studios, film studios, record companies, magazines, publishers, computer companies, marketing firms, public relations firms, and museums. Designers in these organizations work in situations much like those of in-house design departments. A major difference, however, is that the work they produce is much more likely to reach the public.

Third, design companies will vary in size. A small company—not including free-lance designers who work on their own—may have as few as three or four employees. A large-size firm may have well over 100 people on staff. Consider the division of labor in a mid-size firm of thirty people. About one-third of the staff will be designers. There will also be a president and vice-president (these individuals may be designers, copywriters, or marketing specialists, or have some other valuable skill related to the basic task of the firm), a creative director, a few copywriters, perhaps three or four salespersons, as well as a secretary and receptionist. In addition, any number of free-lance artists may be brought in on particular projects. These free-lancers might include a photographer, a typographer, or an illustrator.

Basic Areas of Responsibility

The tasks of designers essentially fall into two broad categories. First, they must create design ideas that can communicate, inform, instruct, and influence. That means that they must think about how a product, service, or idea can be represented visually. Since contemporary society is flooded with visual clutter, however, the key is to present the idea in a way what will catch people's attention. This is no small feat. In order to do that an image or set of images and text must be produced that will arrest the eye and stimulate the mind. This takes a creative and imaginative person; this creativity is what separates good designers from capable design journeymen.

Second, designers must have the technical proficiency necessary to translate their ideas into a finished product that can be sent to production. The graphic designers will handle a number of very specific tasks. One important job, actually a specialization for some designers, involves making "marker comps." This refers to drawings that might be made of people or products in situations. These drawings are made with a felt-tipped marker and are used to represent in rough form what the final design might look like. These drawings are not at all sophisticated or refined in a technical sense. In fact, they often have a rather childlike or stick-figure quality. Their value, however, is that they can effectively communicate design concepts to a client or other members of the design team. At latter stages of the design process, more sophisticated and technically complete comps will be prepared until a final production comp is made ready for printing.

It is also crucial that designers have good language skills and be able to get along well with other people. An ability to communicate visually is not enough. Designers are often engaged in an active social environment that involves interaction with clients, members of their design team, technical support persons, suppliers, and production people. In addition, they must write memos, reports, and business letters in a lucid manner. On occasion, designers may also be called upon to write copy for the work being designed.

Computers

A growing trend is for design work to be done on the computer. Nearly all of the phases of design can now be produced electronically with this rapidly developing technology. This means that designers can bring together the diverse parts of a design project, including images and written copy, and assemble them on the computer screen. The images, copy, background, and other design elements can be moved around quickly and easily. Before computers, for example, changing the typeface on a page layout cost time and money. Now, computers make it possible to experiment with dozens of type styles in a matter of minutes.

Because the various elements can be manipulated with such speed, it is easier to experiment with design variations. Once an initial design has been selected, the computer can be used to make comps that look like the finished product. That enables clients to see what the final product will actually look like. Since these computer-generated comps can be redesigned quickly, it is possible to make rapid changes to satisfy a client's demand for changes. This capability speeds up the process that results in final client approval of the design.

The computer opens up other possibilities for designers. The creation of type styles, for example, can now be done much more easily and quickly on a computer. There is software that is made especially for the design of type. The computer allows a designer to manipulate basic letter designs quickly and easily. Once a style has been developed for just a few letters, the computer can take the design and automatically work that basic idea into the design of all of the letters in the alphabet.

Computers are used in graphic design and advertising design because they enable work to be done quickly and therefore inexpensively. Publishing, in particular, has been more affected by the use of computers for graphic design than any other area. The speed with which design work can be done is of primary importance. Designers can now do page layouts for a magazine in a fraction of the time it used to take.

Computers are also used in the production phase of the process. It is possible, for example, to use the computer to actually make the mechanicals that go to the printer. Many graphic design companies still make mechanicals by hand, but more and more of them are now using the computer. In fact, some design firms will simply transfer their final design work by modem through the telephone line to the printer for final processing. This trend will continue as more and more young designers with computer skills enter the labor force, and as more and more design firms acquire computer technology.

ADVERTISING DESIGN

Advertising design involves a team effort that integrates the talents of a variety of people. For that reason, this is a professional field for those who not only think creatively, but who also have the ability to work cooperatively with other people. Perhaps as much as any of the applied arts, success in advertising requires designers to be sensitive to the cultural themes that they reveal through their ads. Those cultural nuances are what enable advertising designers to convey a visual language with which their target audience can identify.

The Size of Agencies

Most advertising is done in ad agencies. The size of an agency is usually measured by their "billings" (total amount of business) each year. A small agency will have less than 100 million dollars in billings, and a large agency handles 100 million dollars in billings or more. The basic creative team in any size agency will typically include a creative director (the senior level person most responsible for the work that the agency does), art directors (they actually come up with the advertising ideas and will do comps as well), copywriters (they write the words in an advertisement and sometimes are involved in developing basic ideas for the ad campaign), and studio artists (they physically do the layouts and mechanicals for the final copy of the ad). In addition, there may be junior art directors and junior copywriters who sometimes are asked to take care of smaller accounts.

A large agency with a complete staff may also have some of the following artists on staff: graphic designers, typographers, and video specialists. Many agencies, however, will hire illustrators and photographers on a free-lance basis to do special assignments that are not handled routinely by the agency. Small agencies, in particular, may not have a large enough volume of work to employ certain kinds of staff people on an on-going basis. But large agencies hire specialists as well. An ad agency will hire free-lance specialists depending on whether or not the capabilities of the in-house staff are adequate for the technical requirements of a particular job.

Advertising covers a lot of territory. It includes everything from the sign on a child's lemonade stand to the multimillion dollar ad campaigns that are handled by the world's largest agencies. A relatively small advertising job that involves creating an ad for a clothing store to be run in a local newspaper, for example, might be done by an ad agency, but may also be done by a graphic design studio. Larger companies with a local or regional focus will work with ad agencies that handle advertising for those markets. But the advertising done for major national corporations belongs exclusively to the large and prestigious advertising agencies.

These agencies handle in excess of 100 million dollars in billings each year and are responsible for all of the advertising that you see on television and in major national magazines. Most of the advertising is done for companies that sell consumer products, such as cars, razor blades, dishwashing detergent, cookies, fast-food restaurants, personal computers, basketball shoes, deodorant, and beer.

In addition, there are large corporations such as the General Electric Corporation that sell many consumer products, but may that also want to have "goodwill" advertising for the company as a whole. Such advertising may be part of a public relations strategy to maintain the trust and goodwill of the public. Major corporations that sell business-to-business products and services may also do advertising as part of a public relations effort. Advertising may, therefore, pursue a variety of objectives.

Ad Campaigns

An agency will be hired to create an ad campaign. Creating a campaign involves developing a single message or set of messages that are intended to achieve a limited range of objectives through advertising. The messages are usually very simple and straightforward: Volvos are safe cars, Charmin toilet paper is soft, Pop Secret popcorn tastes good. Sometimes there may be a set of related messages that are either implicit or explicit. Commercials for safe driving that are produced for a beer company, for example, may convey a message that explicitly promotes the idea that one should never drive under the influence of alcohol, but that also implies that the beer company is civic-minded and responsive to the needs of the community.

The ad campaign will also involve using a basic message or set of messages in a series of specific advertisements that may appear over a period of time. The advertisements may go through stages that develop different aspects of a message, or that reinforce the message by repeating a familiar advertising idea or approach. The Michelin Tire Company, for example, did a series of advertisements with babies that reinforced the idea that their tires were safe and that responsible people should choose them for their cars. DHL used a "flying" delivery van in a series of ads that suggested that their service was faster than that of their competition.

An ad campaign often will promote a basic message by using an advertising idea in more than one advertising medium. Nike shoes, for example, may use a major sports figure like Michael Jordan in television, magazine, and point-of-sales advertising. This enables the company to reach its target audience in more than one way, thus enabling the advertisements in a variety of media to reinforce one another.

An agency that takes on an advertising assignment will formulate a creative work plan. This will focus on basic information related to the business objective of the client, what action the company wants people to take with respect to their product (to buy it at a store or call for printed information), the message the company wants to tell its customers, what distinctive benefit the product offers, the demographic characteristics of the specific customers that the advertisement will target, as well as information about the customers' preferences and what kind of visual images those individuals will respond to.

Getting a Start

The creative people who work in advertising agencies are often young, and there is a reason for that. The world of advertising is fast-paced, intense, and full of pressure. A lot of money is involved not only in the cost of creating an advertisement, but also in the potential for revenue for the client. Some people describe advertising projects as hit-and-run operations. An advertisement is created, sometimes in a hurried atmosphere. But as soon as that assignment is completed, the creative team picks up another project and the hectic pace begins again.

People also change jobs often in advertising as a way of getting promoted. Companies like to hire individuals who have worked in other agencies. In some ways that is a little like recycling talent within the advertising industry. However, in doing so a new flow of creative energy and ideas makes its way into particular agencies.

The relatively rapid turnover in personnel creates opportunities for individuals who wish to enter the field. Someone who has majored in advertising design in college should have a portfolio full of advertisements and advertising campaigns that show how they think and design. Creativity and being able to carry an idea through phases of the design process are important. Computer skills are also becoming increasingly important, perhaps even essential, for people who want their first job in advertising. Salaries start at a modest level, usually in the range of $18,000 to $19,000 per year, but salary increases come with promotions.

Advertising and Youth Culture

Our culture places such a great emphasis on youth—in this case, people who are in their twenties and thirties. What has been called the "youth culture" has become a dominant theme in our society. This is true, in part, because people in that age range are physically attractive, especially the models who are used in advertisements. Thus, there is a reciprocal relationship between the models used in advertising and the products that are promoted by advertisements. The attractiveness of the models affirm the value of the products, but also the desirability of the products reinforces our perceptions of the attractiveness of the models.

This clearly does not mean that only young people are portrayed in advertisements. Ad agencies know a great deal about the target audience they want to reach for particular products. They know that they need to focus on the right age groups. People who buy Mercedes-Benz automobiles, for example, are often in their forties and fifties, and people who buy laxatives are usually in their fifties and sixties. But if you look at print and television advertising you will see a disproportionate number of young models. A good example of that is the advertisements that are found in *Lear's* magazine for women. This publication is intended for women who are in their forties and above, yet almost all of the advertisements for perfume, clothing, and hair coloring focus on young models who are in their twenties.

INTERIOR DESIGN

Perhaps the first thing to understand about interior design is that it is not the same thing as interior decorating. While it is true that interior designers are responsible for selecting such things as fabrics, furniture, wall and floor covering, accessories, and lighting, that is only one part of what designers do. Interior design is also responsible for preparing plans for the construction of the interior of a building. At its root, interior design has as much to do with knowledge of architecture as it does with knowledge of the decorative arts.

Early on in their educational process, designers learn a variety of skills that enable them to handle technical as well as aesthetic aspects of the profession. Designers are taught how to do the following: architectural drafting, two-dimensional drawn floor plans, reflected ceiling plans (the "floor plan" of the ceiling including lighting), elevations (frontal and side views of an interior space), paraline drawings (three-dimensional drawings using angles to project the walls vertically from a plan), and perspectives that are so central to the interior design process. The use of computer-aided drafting and design (CADD) has made a big impact on the field of interior design. Programming, furniture inventory, plans, elevations, and three-dimensional drawings can now be produced quickly and with great accuracy by computers. More and more designers are learning to use this efficient technology.

Students are also taught such technical knowledge as construction methods and materials, as well as information about basic mechanical, electrical, and plumbing building systems. The aesthetic side of the profession is also important and includes knowledge of a full range of product lines (including fabrics, finishes, furniture, and accessories) that are used to add life to the interior space. Designers also learn about such issues as the history of design styles, color theory, and lighting.

Interior design work falls into two basic categories: contract and residential. Residential work involves designing for the home. It includes everything from apartments and lofts in the city, to suburban residences and vacation homes in the country. In residential design, the client may be one person, a couple, or a family as a whole. This means that the designer must address the needs of a single individual or a number of different people. The home must be thought of as a social unit that centers around interrelated human needs and patterns of living. The residential designer must attend to many different issues that range from the technical and aesthetic to those that are social and psychological. The primary design issues, however, are related to aesthetics and the life-style of the home owner.

Residential designers usually work for themselves, or in partnership with someone else. The residential designer is both a specialist and a jack-of-all-trades. Doing residential interiors requires focused knowledge, skills, and a particular sensitivity to the needs of the residential client. For that reason, it constitutes a distinct and specialized segment of the design market. On the other hand, the residential interior designer is responsible for everything from attracting clients, to design, to purchasing, billing, and bookkeeping. The problems and rewards of residential design are therefore unique and satisfying.

Contract design is more varied and often more complicated because it relates to the health, safety, and welfare of the public. It includes interior design for grocery stores, department stores, restaurants, schools, hospitals, banks, theaters, shopping centers, and professional and business offices of all kinds. There are often complex variables that need to be faced in contract design projects. The aesthetic issues alone can be demanding. For example, the style preference of the diverse kinds of people who pass through an interior space may have to be considered. Or it may be necessary to find a design approach that will be visually comfortable to a more limited and specialized range of people who use an interior space on a daily basis.

Health, safety, and welfare issues are also a major consideration as are issues of accessibility and ease of use for the disabled. Local building and fire codes must also be considered in contract work. The technical and design considerations for particular kinds of clients can be very exacting. For that reason, some clients may want a designer with experience in designing for their particular needs. That is especially true, for example, in the case of hospital or theater design.

Besides aesthetic and safety issues, there are a large number of technical considerations. These include such diverse considerations as the client's electrical requirements for computers and other equipment, acoustical problems, lighting needs, budgetary matters, the psychological effects of color, and the social significance of office size and location. All of these factors will be brought to bear on a contract design project.

There are many different kinds of interior design projects and the various requirements of each one will depend on a number of different factors. First, if the interior project is a part of the architectural design for a whole building, then the architects who design the building may have much to do with designing the interior skeleton of the building. This is especially true if the building is being designed for the needs of a particular client. In that case, interior designers may be more involved with color and the selection of fabrics, floor and wall coverings, furniture, and accessories.

Second, an architect may design a building for a developer that will be leased to tenants at various points after the building has been constructed. In such a case, the building will be designed with empty floor space. An interior design team will then be hired to create the structural configuration or shell of the interior space, but will also be responsible for the aesthetic elements of the design project. The first part of the project will rely on design as well as technical skills and knowledge, and the second part of the design will focus on the decorative arts.

A Typical Contract Project

An interior design project involves a number of phases and will develop over time. This process involves assessing what the client needs, developing a preliminary plan that shows how space for those needs will be organized, preparing drawings that show several aspects of that basic plan in more detail, presenting the plan to the client, coordinating with the client's contractor to establish the budget, and then making sure that the interior construction is done according to the drawings. Let's consider a typical interior design project for an office building that may involve the following tasks (these do not necessarily evolve in a strict linear or time-sequence way).

Programming. The conceptual phase of the project begins by finding out what the client needs and proposing alternative design solutions. Finding out what a client needs is called *programming*. This term refers to the process of assessing a variety of needs and ways the interior space will be used. Thus, programming will focus on the amount of total floor space required for the number of people working in or served by the client company, finding out what kind of space and technical requirements each person has, examining how various individuals interact with one another, as well as determining the organization's need for equipment, storage, offices, meeting space, and circulation (how people move through the interior). This is a very important stage in the life of the project. The design team must accurately assess the client company's current as well as potential needs for space.

Schematic Design. The interior designer will then begin to develop design ideas that are related to the client's program. The designer will begin to sketch out general floor plans based on the various programming requirements of the client, such as office space, work stations, furniture, and circulation routes. As the project moves along, technical drawings (drafting) will be used to indicate the precise measurements and locations for what needs go into the existing space. If a new building is being constructed, some of this work will be designed by architects who specialize in designing interior space. The constraint on interior designers is that, in most states, they cannot do design work that modifies existing structural elements that are used to support the building. Thus, any technical drawings by interior designers that are used to specify interior nonload-bearing construction will not include any work to be done on basic architectural elements in the building.

In addition to allocating and configuring the interior space, the designers must also begin to think about basic aesthetic issues related to color, material, and finishes on walls and floors. Ideas about furniture and accessories will also be discussed during this stage. Such issues must be developed with consideration for the kind of corporate image an organization is trying to promote. A company may want the interior to look very "up-scale" and sophisticated, or it may want to convey a feeling that is more "easy-going" and comfortable to the person on the street. The kind of institutional look that might work for a hospital would probably not be appropriate for a law firm. Each organization will have an image of itself that it would like to have represented in the atmosphere or character of its interior. Thus, the job of the interior designer is to find a visual language that an organization can use to symbolically communicate a sense of itself to its employees and those that it serves.

Design Development. Once the designers have determined the client's program, prepared schematic drawings that show the interior space, considered the image the organization is trying to project, developed a few aesthetic approaches, and also understood the client's budget constraints, the task is then to develop a specific design scheme.

At this point, the designer will move beyond general technical and aesthetic considerations to consider specific details. Precise floor plans will be laid out that show exactly what the floor plan will be and where the various furniture and accessories will be located in that space. In addition, the specific kinds of product lines and colors for wall and floor finishes, ceiling, lighting, fabrics, furniture, and accessories for the interior will be determined. The designers will then make a presentation of the design to the client who will then either agree to the design proposal, or, more typically, will ask for particular refinements. Once a design as been approved and budget is finalized, the project can move forward.

The design development phase of the project involves taking the design proposal and making it real. Once the technical and aesthetic issues have been determined, a bid will be sent out to contractors who will do the various kinds of work required. A bid will also be sent out to dealers who carry the various product lines. Once the client has selected from among the bids, orders for the various design products are then placed.

Construction Documents. The construction document includes technical drawings that show how the interior space is to be constructed, and specifications that indicate exactly what kind of design products will be put into the interior. The construction document legally binds all the parties involved. The drawings, for example, may indicate where a cabinet or work station must be placed, and the specifications will indicate exactly what kind of cabinet and work station are to be installed. The specifications also indicate exactly what furniture, lighting, and so forth are to be used in the project.

Construction Administration. The interior design team will be responsible for quality control. In particular they must be sure that the construction documents are being followed exactly, which means making field inspections until the project has been completed.

Merging the Technical and Aesthetic

Not all students who enter college to study interior design are aware that there are two sides to interior design work. As the previous paragraphs have shown, interior design is an interesting blend of technical issues, such as those related to architectural drawings and knowledge of construction methods and material, with aesthetic issues, such as those related to color, fabrics, furniture, and lighting. Anyone wishing to understand the field must be clear about the full range of requirements for the profession.

The Size of Design Firms

As with other kinds of design fields, the size of interior design firms can affect the range of work that a young designer will do. In larger firms, design tasks tend to be more specialized. There are some large firms, however, where designers tend not to specialize. In those cases, designers are asked to handle a variety of tasks so that more work can be done by fewer people. This allows companies to reduce their labor costs. In either case, however, a designer who is just starting out may spend most of the time drafting floor plans or elevations. It is also not likely that a young designer will have any contact with clients unless a project is small.

Interior designers often work with architects. In fact, many of the larger architectural firms will have an interior design department. In such cases architects and designers work together on a single project. That is especially true when a firm is hired to design an entire building. In such cases, the division of labor is such that the architects will design the interior and exterior skeleton, and interior designers will be responsible for selecting the interior colors, fabrics, finishes, furniture, and accessories. In large renovation projects, the plans for interior construction may be done by architects or designers depending on the nature of the work required.

In smaller firms with a few designers, there is a greater chance for young designers to get more varied work experience. Each member of a small firm may have to pitch in and do a variety of tasks. A designer will still have to learn the ropes and spend time doing the less interesting though important work of drafting, but may be able to move on to more varied tasks sooner than would be the case in a large firm.

FASHION DESIGN

There is perhaps no other applied art field that is so deeply connected to the everyday lives of real people than fashion design. Fashion design is responsible for the clothing that we wear at home, school, and work.

What we wear is just as relevant when we go to a baseball game as when we go to the ballet. Clothing not only keeps us warm and protects us from the elements, it also helps shape who we are in a social and psychological sense. It forms a visible basis for our social identity.

Fashion design is one part of a larger network of industry relationships that also includes manufacturing and sales. Although fashion designers are primarily responsible for the actual design of clothing, they must also be mindful of whether standard manufacturing methods are suited to the materials and patterns of particular designs. They are also intimately concerned with the problems and prospects related to sales. In fact, design decisions are largely determined by a consideration of what will and will not sell.

Fashion design employs a large number of people. Although there are some free-lance designers, most people have staff positions in fashion design firms or companies that manufacture clothing. The center of the clothing industry in the United States is New York City, but clothing is manufactured in nearly all large-size cities. For that reason, fashion design provides a variety of good career opportunities.

Positions in Fashion Design

The process of designing clothing develops in a series of stages that evolve from design ideas to the production process. There are specific positions that are responsible for each stage. The head designer is responsible for creating fashion ideas and developing a line of clothing. The head designer will either make sketches of basic ideas or will describe design ideas to an illustrator or assistant designer who will produce the sketches. The designer must also select the fabrics and colors that are needed for each garment. In addition to helping out with the initial design process, assistant designers make accurate patterns that are used to translate the designer's working sketch into an actual garment. Assistant designers may also spend time looking for just the right button or trim for a particular garment that is being developed. This kind of research is important to creating a finished look.

Once the basic design idea has been sketched out and a pattern has been made, it is given to a sample cutter who cuts material for the sample garment that will be shown to buyers. Then the sample maker constructs and hand finishes the sample. The first sample is made as complete as it can be and includes such things as buttonholes, trim, and other details. The sample maker works closely with the fashion designer to make any necessary changes or adjustments to the garment. Once the sample garment is complete, it is ready to be shown to wholesale buyers. After orders are placed, the garment is ready to be manufactured.

Design Considerations

Fashion designers must take into account a variety of considerations related to their design ideas. Some of those considerations are technical, but most of them focus on the needs, tastes, and buying patterns of various categories of consumers. Taking these human factors into account helps establish the marketability of clothing and therefore has everything to do with the design process.

Some technical considerations are related to the manufacturing process. Certain fabrics, for example, may be too delicate for particular kinds of construction methods. Other technical considerations are related to the characteristics of fabrics and how they will be used. Designers need to know which fabrics will hold a crease, which will be comfortable in warm weather, and which will stand up to use in a washer and dryer. Each of these fabric characteristics is essential in selecting material for certain kinds of garments or garments designed for particular seasons.

Perhaps the most interesting design considerations are those based on a social and psychological understanding of people. There are several equally important factors that must be taken into account in the design process. These include sex, gender, age, region of the country, season of the year, the intended uses of clothing, and price points. Such factors have to be taken into account by the designer because they are important to the customer. These factors are "designed into" clothing as a basic part of marketing strategies.

The most basic design considerations are sex and gender. Sex refers to physical differences between men and women, and gender refers to cultural manifestations related to sex. Almost all clothing is designed for the explicit difference in the way men and women dress. It is a difference that is found in clothing for all age groups and almost all occasions.

In college, where men and women appear to often dress alike, gender may not seem to be a significant factor. That impression is not altogether correct, however. There are subtle yet important differences in the design of such items as jeans and sneakers for men and women. These differences are especially important to college-age individuals who are often concerned about their attractiveness to members of the opposite sex. Physical differences between men and women are also significant from a design point of view because of their differences in height, weight, and shape. Thus, both the physical differences related to sex and the cultural differences related to gender need to be factored into fashion design.

Age is another basic factor that is related to design issues such as size, color, and style. People grow rapidly from the time they are infants to their late teens. Fashion design must take the size differences related to age into account. But they need to take changes in the shape of the human figure into account as well. Men and women begin to change their shape as they get older and designers who want to sell to an older market must take those changes into account. The figure is not the only thing to change. Designers also need to pay attention to taste and style preferences in clothing that are related to changes in life-style. Generally speaking, people want to wear clothing that reflects what they have aspired to become. Conversely, they do not want to be reminded of what they are no longer able to be.

Regions of the country and seasons of the year are also relevant design considerations. The kind of clothing as well as the choice of fabric, style, and color will vary depending on where in the United States the clothing will be worn. In New England, upstate New York, and northern states like Michigan and Minnesota, clothing styles and fabrics need to be suited to cool or cold weather during much of the year. In the south and southwest, as well as in California, clothing needs to be light and is often colorful. Similarly, clothing needs will vary between summer and winter, especially in parts of the country that have significant temperature shifts between the seasons.

Designers need to be aware of these considerations, but do not necessarily have to resolve the fashion issues related to each one whenever they begin a new design. That is because many designers will focus only on one established market area or range of areas such as "misses," "teens" or "active sportswear" within a particular price range. In cases where the selection of a specialty area has resolved basic design issues, the designer will focus on matters related to color, style changes, or season.

The "price point" or cost of a garment is critically important from both a manufacturing and a marketing point of view. Customers expect the clothing of particular manufacturers to fall within a fairly narrow price range. If price points vary too much, the clothing will not sell. That means that designers must select material and styles that will keep the manufacturing costs where they need to be. It is also the case that the designers will offer a few different lines, each with a set price-point range, within their overall collection.

The Cycle of Fashion Design

There are resource publications that help designers think about colors and styles for the coming seasons. These publications come from companies that forecast or predict coming trends based on their analysis of changes that take place in style over time. The forecasts which are presented in periodicals such as *Tobé* and *Here and There* provide the fashion industry with loose sketches of what researchers believe will be in style during the next season. These forecasting publications give fashion designers a common frame of reference for long-range design planning.

People generally buy new clothing before old clothing wears out. A primary reason for this is that they want to keep up with changes in style. These changes are tied to a trickle-down trend in fashion development.

Often, style changes begin with the most exclusive fashion designers like Karl Lagerfeld, Gianni Versace, or Gianfranco Ferré. As soon as the newest fashions from these designers come out, they are "knocked off" (exact copies are made) by other manufacturers who make less-expensive copies sometimes with interpretations added. The knock-off is sold either right away or during the next season for much less money. Other less-expensive knock-off versions of the garment may be sold perhaps two or even three seasons after the original design was shown. By the time a style trend has reached the lowest end of the market it will have been abandoned by couture designers who will have developed new fashion trends.

It may take the top designers a few seasons to exhaust the possibilities of a style trend. In the mid-1980s, for example, shoulder pads were introduced into exclusive fashions for women. These shoulder pads were small in size during their first season. But when they sold well in the expensive boutiques, top designers enlarged them over the course of a few seasons. By the time they reached the bottom of the fashion market, they had been abandoned by the name designers. This downward movement of style and the development of new styles at the top of the fashion world is in large measure an economic consequence of the buying patterns of status conscious consumers. Consumers typically want to acquire the symbols of those in a higher social class, and at the same time want to move away from symbols of those in a lower class.

CHAPTER 6

APPLIED ART AS A CAREER II: FREE-LANCE WORK

One of the most distinctive characteristics of free-lance work is the tension between a particular kind of independence and the burden of self-reliance for the individual. As we have seen, fine artists face this kind of duality. It is also a condition of some applied art fields, especially illustration and photography. This means that free-lance works best for those artists who find that the working conditions of this kind of employment are able to satisfy their social, psychological, and creative needs.

The term *free-lance* refers to professional work that is done without long-term or exclusive commitments to one employer. A free-lance artist or designer actually runs an independent business that sells services (or products) to a number of different clients. This means that free-lance professionals must have many talents and abilities. They must set up their own studio, order their own equipment and supplies, do their own public relations wok, get their own clients, set and maintain schedules, contract out work that they may need to have done for a project, keep records, handle billing, and take care of accounts receivable. They also need to actually do the art or design work that they get paid to do.

ILLUSTRATION

Illustrators produce drawings and paintings that convey information or make an idea clear. For that reason, their work is usually representational and sometimes has a very lifelike quality. Some illustration, however, relies much more on the artist's imagination to make a familiar image more interesting and eye catching. Or an illustrator may take an abstract idea or a human emotion and show it visually. The needs of the client will dictate the specific nature of the illustration. In either case, however, the work that is produced will be similar to representational or figurative fine art. As you will recall from Chapter 3, this kind of art presents a naturalistic rendering of the real word. The image looks like the thing being portrayed.

The object being portrayed and the image, however, are not the same thing. There is a very "realistic" painting of a tobacco pipe by the French artist René Magritte that is entitled "This is not a pipe." By using this title, the artist calls our attention to the fact that the painting is not a pipe, but rather a picture of a pipe. The idea from this painting and its title is instructive. Although this painting is an example from the world of fine art, it reminds us that illustrative renderings will always be an interpretation of the object being produced. In all cases, the artist adds a creative or distinctive touch to the image being produced. Therefore, the fact that an illustration is made in response to a client's or art director's needs does not keep it from being art. It simply means that it is not the same as fine art.

Illustrations are uniquely suited as a means of representing certain kinds of images that cannot be shown through photography. Perhaps the most obvious example would be images of people who were alive before photography was invented. If a client needs a picture of Shakespeare, for example, it has to be an illustration. Or if an image is required for a place that is hard to photograph, such as the surface of a planet, a very deep part of the ocean floor, or an imaginary landscape, then an illustration will probably be called for. There are many such needs that only illustration can satisfy.

Staff Jobs

It is not quite correct to say that all illustrators work on a free-lance basis. There are a few illustrators who have staff positions in a company or who work in firms that only handle illustration. A company that manufactures consumer products, for example, may have people on staff who can illustrate the product and the way it should be used. These drawings are usually technical in nature. Certain publications such as *Popular Mechanics* or the grade-school magazine called *Highlights* require a lot of illustration and may therefore have an illustrator on staff. Greeting card companies such as Hallmark Cards or American Greetings will have illustrators on staff. There are also a few illustrators who start in newspapers by making weather charts and economic graphs, and may then go on to illustrate advertising. Beyond these rather limited situations, however, most work is done by free-lance or independent illustrators.

Editorial Illustration

The work of illustrators falls into two basic categories: editorial and commercial. The differences between them are related to how much creative freedom the artist has. Editorial work is more interpretive and therefore requires more artistic individuality. This is perhaps why artists are more interested in doing this kind of illustration assignment even though the pay is less than it might be for commercial illustration.

Editorial illustrations are found in magazine articles, magazine and book covers, newspapers, and books. They attempt to portray something that has been written. The image can be rendered in a direct and literal way, or, as is more frequently the case, in a creative and visually interesting way, depending on the nature of the text being illustrated and publication in which the text appears. An illustrator doing a piece for a magazine article, for example, will read the article and then try to capture a central idea or theme in the illustration. An art director working for the magazine who hires the illustrator may give the illustrator an idea of what kind of image is desired. Even in that case, however, the illustration will be very much related to the written text. An illustrator with a prominent reputation may have more freedom to interpret the ideas that need to be represented visually.

Commercial Illustration

Commercial illustration involves drawings or paintings that are used in corporate manuals, annual reports, brochures, text books, employee publications, direct-mail campaigns, television commercials, animation, and advertising. Such illustration is not used to accompany the kind of text that would be found in stories, articles, or book covers. Therefore, the style requirements are different. This kind of illustration is usually less interpretive and more realistic.

Another important area is art work that is intended to be displayed at the "point of purchase" in retail stores. This would involve an illustration that is used to catch the consumer's eye at the point where the product is be purchased. Such illustrations may help reinforce a television commercial, suggest a need for the product, or help link the product with a particular segment of the market. A good example of "point of purchase" illustrations might be the Happy Meals cartoon characters that are displayed at McDonald's restaurants. The requirements for producing these standardized images are so stringent that the McDonald's Corporation actually has manuals that show illustrators how to draw such cartoon characters as Ronald McDonald, the Hamburgler, and the French Fry Guys.

A Typical Assignment

What is required of a typical illustration job? Let's say that a regional Coca-Cola distributor wants an ad agency to produce an eye-catching display ad that will be used to promote the sale of Coke at grocery stores. The art director, copywriter, and creative director from the agency meet to develop an idea for the ad. The art director will make a few comps (design sketches for the ad) and then sell the idea to the client. In this particular case, the art director wants the display ad to have an illustration that will be used to highlight the product. The idea involves using an illustration that shows cans of Coke bursting out of a tub of ice.

The art director already has examples of the work of a few illustrators on file. These illustrators will be asked to submit a bid on how much they will charge to produce the required illustration. Based on the bids and the illustration samples, the client will then give the agency the go-ahead to hire the illustrator. The illustrator will then take the comps, some photographs of the product and any other visual material from the ad agency. In addition, the illustrator may want to find a tub or take a photo of a tub to use as a reference for the drawing.

A "tissue drawing" will then be made that shows in outline form what the finished drawing will look like. The art director will see the drawing and either approve it or ask for changes. If major changes are required that go beyond what was specified in the preliminary comp sketches, the illustrator may charge more for the additional work. Once the drawing is approved, it will be transferred to the paper on which the final drawing is produced. This paper (or other material) is called a "board." The next step involves making a very precise painting of what the art director asked for: cans of Coke busting from a tub full of ice. At this point the art director will either accept the painting as it is or will ask for changes. When the painting is finally accepted, the illustrator is no longer involved in the project. The illustration then becomes integrated into the display ad.

The same process is used to produce illustrations for print advertising in magazines and newspapers. This is a large area in illustration. One reason why fees for such work are relatively large is that companies are willing to spend a lot of money to advertise their products. Advertising increases sales and therefore increases revenues for the company. Illustrators contribute to that income-producing system.

Stock Agencies

There is a new trend in the marketing and distribution of illustrations. Previously, all illustrations were commissioned for a particular assignment. An art director or client would have a specific need, and the illustrator would produce the desired image. Now there are companies that have illustrations on file that can be sold through a catalog. These companies are called stock agencies.

One of the largest stock agencies is called The Image Bank, which is headquartered in New York. This company has over sixty branches worldwide and sells both photographs and illustrations. The illustration division is relatively new to the company. Currently, The Image Bank works with about 200 illustrators. Each artist will have somewhere between 25 and 100 illustrations or more on file.

The library at each agency will have a large number of such diverse illustration categories as famous people from the past, the inside of machines, or historical settings. These are the categories from which clients choose the various images they need. As we have seen, many of these images can only be produced through illustration. The most recent trend in images is for illustrations that represent concepts rather than people, places, or things. A client may contact a stock agency that handles illustrations and ask for an image that represents such concepts as "competitiveness," "winning," "hope," or "human energy." Such conceptual categories give illustrators who produce work for stock agencies creative license to translate interesting ideas into concrete images.

Illustration for Children's Books

No matter what your age, you probably remember a favorite book from childhood. The fond memories will undoubtedly include the wonderful illustrations that were a part of the book. Actually, children's books and the illustrations that go with them are of relatively recent origin. The reason for this is that the concept of "childhood" is only a few hundred years old. Prior to that, children were perceived as being young in age and small in size, but not socially or psychologically distinct from adults. Only in the last few hundred years have children been thought of as having special developmental and educational needs. Children's books have come about, in part, because of that change. *Children and Books* by Zena Sutherland and May Hill Arbuthnot provides an excellent historical overview of children's books and their illustrations. It is well worth looking at not only for its historical frame of reference but also for the delightful book illustrations that it presents.

Children's books are wonderful from an illustrator's point of view because they require a high degree of creativity and imagination. The requirements for illustrations will vary depending on the age of the children for whom the book was written. For very young children, books will have many illustrations and relatively little text. For older children, the illustrations can be more complex and more inventive. In either case, illustrations for children focus on something that is immediately recognizable and therefore something that is fundamentally human.

Illustrations are related to what the book is about. They focus on parts of the story that are visually strong, include references to the main characters, or provide information about location. These illustrations may also add something to the story that is not actually present in the written text. A wonderful example is a book called *Agatha's Featherbed* by Laura Seeley. The story is about geese who want to get their feathers back from a kindly old woman with long gray hair who has unintentionally been sleeping on their feathers in her featherbed. In the illustrations, the old woman is shown as having eight cats, even though there is nothing in the story to indicate that fact. The cats are an added dimension that makes the character in the story more interesting and visually appealing.

The publication of children's books is a growing area. Sometimes an illustrator will team up with a writer and present a finished product to the publisher. Or a publisher will have a written story and will hire an artist to do the illustrations. Another possibility is that an artist will write the story and do the illustrations. In many cases, this is the most preferable option. In addition to issues of creative control and professional satisfaction that come from doing both parts of a book, there is an significant economic advantage. The royalties from each book will average about 10 percent of its retail price. If a writer and illustrator work on the book together, they will split the profits. Someone who is both author and artist will get full share of the royalties.

Getting a Start

Again, we find that there is a difference between the job market in New York City and in other parts of the country. In New York there are no illustration studios, which means that all of the illustration work is done by free-lance artists. The result is that the market of work is very competitive, and yet at the same time very democratic. This is because the single most compelling factor in getting illustration work is the quality of one's art work. As the prominent New York illustrator and fine artist Marshal Arisman has said, "It all comes down to the portfolio and what's in it." Therefore, a young illustrator just out of college with an excellent portfolio can get work. But, as Arisman emphasizes, there are many illustrators out there who are competing for assignments so the work in one's portfolio must be truly first-rate.

Years ago one had to live in New York to get the best illustration assignments that came from the top advertising agencies. That is no longer the case. Today, it is possible to send samples or slides of work to the art directors at magazines. The difficulty with that approach, however, is that a magazine will tend to prefer a particular style that compliments the content of the publication, or that will be appreciated by its readers. Therefore, it is important to have a very good idea of the kind of illustrations that a magazine is likely to use before sending samples of one's illustrations.

Another route for getting work, particularly in smaller cities, is the art representative or "rep." These are people who save illustrators the leg-work of going to the different ad agencies and showing their work. Art reps, however, are sometimes reluctant to take on illustrators who are just beginning. Unless an illustrator has a proven record of reliability and performance, the rep may not want to take a chance in making a recommendation to an ad agency. If the illustrator cannot produce work quickly enough or is difficult to work with, the judgment of the rep who promoted that person would be called into question by the art director at the ad agency. That is a situation that an art rep cannot afford. After all, the business of being a rep is also competitive and they do not work for free. Reps get between 25 percent and 30 percent of the price of the illustration project as compensation for their efforts.

Computers

Computers are making inroads into illustration slowly but steadily. The primary reason for this trend is that computers can simulate some media better than others. In the past, computers could simulate paint and pastel, for example, but could not simulate pencil or ink drawings as well. It is possible to do drawings with a computer, but the final product is not always easier or quicker to produce than it is by hand. That is likely to change in the future, however, as more sophisticated computer software becomes available.

The work that is done on a computer using pastel or paint simulation is excellent. In fact, you can no longer tell very easily when certain kinds of illustrations have been done by hand or by computer. Such computer techniques are used in illustration for television. They are especially useful for animation, which requires the rapid production of evolving illustrations.

PHOTOGRAPHY

Photography is one of the most prevalent of the applied art areas. Photographic images are everywhere. You can find them in magazines, newspapers, newsletters, catalogs, brochures, book covers, annual corporate reports, textbooks, restaurant menus, calendars, postcards, billboards, product packaging, store windows, and display advertising. Even baseball cards use photographs. While there are a few photographic images that are famous and seem to be a permanent part of our cultural heritage, most photographs are rather disposable. Once they are used for a particular commercial purpose they disappear from our visual landscape.

There are also more cameras available now than ever before. The high quality of the technology and the low price of basic equipment make the medium accessible to a large number of people. There is still a world of difference, however, between an amateur with a camera and the world of professional photography. That difference is a consequence of the consistently high quality of professional work, as well as the economic and occupational circumstances that characterize the field.

Staff Positions

There are not many staff positions for photographers. Newspapers and news services such as the AP hire photographers. There are also specialty magazines such as *National Geographic* that have photographers on staff. But job such as these are scarce. In most cases, a magazine or any other business or individual who needs a photograph will either hire an independent photographer or will buy a photograph from a stock house.

Photographic Studios

Many independent photographers own their own studios. If they shoot photographs in their studios, they will have a space set up with controlled lighting and other equipment in place. Location photographers who travel on assignments may also have a studio. In that case, however, the studio will function more as a business office and base of operations than a place where photography is actually done. A studio may also include a darkroom for photographic processing. But in many cases, especially where color photography is involved, film will be processed and printed in laboratories that specialize in work done by professional photographers.

From a business point of view, a studio can be both an asset and a liability. The advantage in having a studio is that it can give clients the sense of the photographer's permanence and stability. A studio can also be a convenient place for conducting business; it can also be used for storing supplies and equipment. But a studio is also a hungry mouth that needs to be fed every month. Regardless of how much business is coming into the studio, the rent, phone bills, utilities, and insurance have to be paid on time.

Most photography studios are small. Even the studios of internationally known photographers may have as few as three or four people working in them. The reason for the small size is that a single person can produce a photograph. By contrast, graphic design or advertising design may require the skills of a number of people. A photographer will need an assistant or two, plus someone who can take care of bookkeeping and scheduling. In some cases, a photographer may have a "second shooter" who can also do some of the more basic photography or work on small photographic assignments. Beyond that, not much more is needed. On those occasions where a large amount of equipment is required for a location shoot, free-lance assistants can be hired for any number of days or weeks.

Thus, while independent photographers may have their own studios, they still function as free-lance artists especially from the point of view of art directors that hire them to shoot a particular assignment. These photographers work for themselves and do not have a permanent or exclusive employment relationship with a single company. Independent photographers will work on many assignments during the year. The assistants who work with photographers can be thought of as having staff jobs, but these are typically not career positions. Instead, they are considered to be something rather like apprenticeship positions. Such positions are useful for learning but no one wants or expects to work at them for long. Free-lance assistants are paid on a per diem basis and earn around $75 to $100 a day in smaller cities and more in larger cities. Most assistants aspire to have their own studio.

Like illustrators, many independent photographs have photo reps who show their work to ad agencies and design firms. This is a valuable yet time-consuming service that many photographers need. They rely on photo reps because they are typically unable to devote enough of their own time and attention to various marketing strategies.

Specialization

Today photography is highly specialized. Individuals may specialize in photographing people, food, products, architecture, sports, automobiles, and fashion. Specialization has evolved out of the photographer's need to find work in a competitive market. It is a way of developing an expertise that art directors can turn to when they need to feel confident about the outcome of a photographer's work. Photographers may move from one specialization to another, but they generally stay within a familiar range.

Advertising photography involves all of the work done for print advertising that you find in magazines, newspapers, and also in point-of-purchase displays. This kind of work is done as part of a creative team that is coordinated by an art director at an advertising agency. The art director will typically specify what is required of the photograph. Experienced photographers who have been working with a particular agency or art director for a period of time may be able to make creative recommendations. But oftentimes the photographer is hired to execute an idea that has come from someone else.

Some photography can have the kind of glamour that people sometimes associate with the profession. But many of the more lucrative assignments have little or no glamour. Catalog work is a case in point. There are companies that sell industrial or commercial supplies, for example, that require catalogs that show their products. These might involve such products as industrial lighting, heavy earth-moving equipment, small power tools, residential carpeting, or toilet seats. These products may not have much sex appeal, but they all need to be photographed. An on-going relationship with a company that requires a lot of catalog photography can be an excellent bread-and-butter account for a photographer.

Stock Agencies

Earlier, we looked at the recent trend in stock illustration, which is, in fact, an outgrowth of stock agencies that handle photography. The

Image Bank, for example, worked only with photographs and then very recently added illustrations. The photography side of stock agencies works the same way that illustration does. The stock agency will sell its photographs to anyone who needs a particular kind of image. These photographs are usually generic images of mountains, sunsets, street scenes, dairy farms, fans at a ballpark, or people at the beach. Other broad categories include travel, food, medical, underwater, geography, or industry. Each broad area is further broken down into subcategories. Industry, for example, may include such areas as computer production, steel manufacturing, or fiber optics.

These images are used in magazines, advertisements, and textbooks. A sociology textbook, for example, may require photographs of extended families (mother, father, children, and relatives) from several different cultures. Stock companies will have hundreds of photographs in that category from which textbook editors can choose.

Stock photographs are often used when it is not practical to hire a photographer for a specific assignment. When there is an unexpectedly tight deadline, for example, a stock photograph can be obtained in a day or less. Or when it is too expensive to hire a photographer to fly from Chicago to shoot a street scene in Paris, a stock agency will have a large number of Parisian street scenes from which a client can choose.

The Image Bank has over 5 million photographic transparencies from about 450 photographers in stock in their sixty-two offices. The number is not quite as large as it may seem, however, because each office will have a duplicate of the many of the photographs that the other offices have. Nonetheless, the agency has a very large number of images on file.

Photographs are sold on consignment. The photographer and the agency each get 50 percent of the price of each photograph that is sold. The sale price of a photograph will depend on how it is to be used. If a photograph is going to be published in a small in-house newsletter, the lowest price for the image would be $150 to $200. On the other hand, the cost of a photograph that is going to be used for an American Express marketing brochure that will be mailed to 500,000 people may be as high as $10,000 or more.

It is not easy to get a start in stock photography largely because of the time and expense involved in developing a large enough portfolio. A stock agency may require a photographer to submit a minimum of 5,000 photographs. That enormous number of photographs represents a very large investment of time spent shooting as well as cost in film and processing. This is especially true since only some of the photographs taken in each roll of film will have the kind of quality the photographer and stock agency are looking for.

Getting Started

The typical starting position is that of photographer's assistant, but getting that first job is tough. The key, however, is persistence and willingness to work hard. There are many stories about individuals who were willing to ask for a job as an assistant with a particular photographer repeatedly. In time, the photographer became sufficiently impressed by the display of commitment and determination to give the person a chance. Such persistence is good preparation for the kind of drive necessary to make it in the competitive world of professional photography.

A strong recommendation from a faculty member at an art college can help in getting a start as an assistant. An internship in which a student works with a photographer as part of his or her college education can also serve as a valuable entrance into a professional work situation.

The duties of a photographer's assistant involve a variety of menial chores. They include scheduling photographic sessions, setting up studio shots, hiring models, loading film, and some lab work, such as film processing and ordering supplies. Assistants who work for "location" photographers will also do a lot of hauling and setting up of equipment at various locations. After working for a while, an assistant may be given small assignments that the photographer does not want to handle. These provide excellent experience and can pave the way for other assignments.

In addition to being hired on as permanent assistants, many young photographers work as free-lance assistants when photographers need their help for a particular job. Such work lacks permanence and stability, but can provide great opportunities to learn. Free-lance assistants are exposed to a wide variety of photographic assignments, locations, professional equipment, aesthetic approaches and techniques, professional work habits, professional settings, and business skills. Free-lance assistants are often hired to help with location assignments that sometimes require travel to foreign countries. The assignments will last anywhere from a few days to a few weeks and then an assistant will hire on with another photographer.

Some photographers get their start by working in a photographic laboratory that processes and prints color as well as black and white film. Such labs are set up to handle work that comes in from professional photographers who ordinarily do not print their own color work. These professional labs have high standards and hire individuals who are well trained and technically competent. The salary range for beginning lab technicians is $15,000 to $17,000.

The quality of a young photographer's portfolio is often not as important as a willingness to help and do work. This is especially true if one starts a career in the field by being an assistant. Other attributes that are important include reliability, self-motivation, and a cooperative attitude. The quality of the portfolio becomes more significant later when a photographer begins to get work on his or her own. At that point, art directors and clients will want to look at samples of photography.

Beginning opportunities for photographers also exist by aiming for free-lance assignments that may not be so competitive. Small magazines, for example, that are often local or regional in scope and that cater to a select readership make use of images to accompany text in much the way that larger national publications do. In addition, small public relations firms need photographs of their clients or aspects of their clients' organizations. Companies like these as well as larger advertising agencies and publications of all kinds sometimes have a "drop-off" policy that allows photographers to leave their work to be reviewed and picked up at a later time.

Setting Up a Studio

Setting up a studio and working as an independent photographer takes a lot of capital. The major costs include all of the equipment necessary for either studio or location work. In addition to several kinds of cameras and many kinds of lenses, a photographer will need lighting equipment, tripods, and light meters. In addition, anyone who sets up a studio may need to be able to pay rent and other bills for the studio space for at least six months before a sufficient amount of work comes in. The total set-up cost for a studio may be anywhere from $100,000 to $150,000 and up depending on the city in which the studio is located. There are very few young professionals who have the financial resources to be on their own right out of college.

Computers

Taking a photograph is only one part of a process that leads to the finished product. There are many darkroom techniques used during the printing of a photograph that add to its final look. These darkroom techniques are now being done by a computer, and they are playing a significant role in professional photography.

Once a photograph has been taken and printed, the image can be "scanned" into a computer. This refers to a process by which a image is placed on an electronic scanner that looks much like a small copy machine. Light from the scanner passes over the image in a way similar to what happens in a copy machine process and then feeds it into a computer. The computer then takes the information it receives as light and transforms and stores it as digital information. Once it is inside the computer, the digital information can be manipulated and the "photograph" can be changed in a variety of interesting ways.

Thus, the process called photo retouching that used to be done by hand in the darkroom can now be done electronically by the computer. Some of the photographs that you can now see in magazines have been manipulated in this way. Computers can add "grain" or that sandy-looking quality you sometimes see in photographs. Or they can add an "antique" look which gives a photograph a somewhat soft and golden appearance. They can also make images look as though they have been subjected to a swirling process that can give them a dreamlike look. Once the desired effect has been created, the computer can then print the photograph as a physical image using a laser printer. The end result is a computer printout of a real photograph.

Perhaps the most interesting development on the horizon is digital photography. Instead of using film that records light, cameras will use computer disks that transform light from the camera's lens into digital information that is recorded on a computer disk. This allows images to be stored on the disk electronically. Once the disk and its digital information are fed into the computer, the "photograph" is ready for electronic retouching. The computer can then print out a photograph in final form.

CHAPTER 7

TEACHING ART AND ART THERAPY

Teaching art and art therapy are closely related professional fields that have much in common. Their values lie in the benefit that people derive from the process of making art. The creative and expressive nature of making art has educational and therapeutic potential. These fields offer excellent career opportunities for individuals who are committed to art and who like to work with people.

Teaching art involves the ability to bring out the special gift of visual creativity in people who already possess it. This can be an enormously satisfying experience, and one whose value is widely recognized. Art teachers are respected for what they contribute to the individual, as well as to the community as a whole. Because of its recognized value, art teachers are relatively well paid.

The majority of teaching art falls roughly into two major categories: public school teaching and teaching on the postsecondary level. The first category involves teaching art in kindergarten through senior year in high school (K–12). The second category involves teaching art in colleges and universities where the focus is more on professional training objectives. On occasion, there may be some occupational movement between the two categories as individuals move from one sector into the other. But for the most part, individuals who specialize in one area remain there throughout their careers. This is true in large part because of the different professional training requirements in each educational setting.

Art therapy also provides especially attractive career opportunities for individuals who enjoy art and derive satisfaction from helping others. In fact, the essence of this growing field lies in helping by involving others in art. The art therapist works in a variety of institutional settings as part of a therapeutic team that is capable of addressing the physical, emotional, and psychiatric problems of clients. Individuals who work in this field must be knowledgeable about the expressive and communicative functions of art. That knowledge must also be integrated with theories of human psychology and behavior, as well as with the practical aspects of art making.

ART EDUCATION

The term *art education* usually refers to a very specific occupational area that involves teaching art within the public school system. The two fundamental subdivisions in art education are based on the distinction between elementary (grammar school) and secondary education (high school). Since art education in the public school system is supported by public funds, its agenda is to educate all children in art, not simply those who are assumed to have special talent.

The resources for and commitments to art education are somewhat mixed. One the one hand, all fifty states certify teaching specialists in art on the elementary and secondary school level. Virtually all schools or school systems have a visual arts program. This means that employment prospects are excellent for art teachers who have just graduated from college. On the other hand, a new teacher may not always find the teaching resources for art to be as plentiful as they would like them to be within the school. Such things as a specialized classroom for teaching art, a written art curriculum, a full stock of art supplies and equipment, as well as adequate funding for art programs cannot always be counted on.

Nonetheless, there is good reason to be optimistic about the prospects for art education. A privately funded organization, the Getty Center for Education in the Arts, has been a major source of ideas and energy.

Through its efforts and the efforts of other professional organizations, such as the National Art Education Association, there have been ongoing attempts to promote values, ideas, research, leadership, advocacy, curriculum development, and professional development services necessary for the continued growth of the field. Together, these efforts point to a general social awareness of and commitment to the role art in elementary and secondary education.

Understanding the fundamental rationale for art education helps to explain the positive contribution it makes to the individual and society, and also explains what lies at the heart of the profession for art educators. The objectives of art education say something basic about what motivates individuals to pursue this career path, and what the practice of the profession entails.

General Educational Philosophy

Art education is part of a general educational philosophy in the United States. Among other things, this philosophy has sought to provide people with the learning experiences they need to be fully developed individuals and to appreciate the world in which they live. A variety of educational goals have been articulated for public education under this banner. These include such broadly based objectives as fostering the growth and enrichment of the individual and establishing cultural links between the individual and other members of the community. Art education is consistent with both of these objectives.

Enriching the Individual

The future of children is influenced by what they learn at an early age. This is true not only with regard to specific knowledge and skills they acquire, but also with regard to the basic capacities they develop. These capacities grow in value, much like economic investments. Art education expands the child's capacity for thought. It stimulates the imagination, brings to life a variety of concrete problem-solving experiences, and activates the potential for personal creativity. Early experiences with art also increase a child's capacity to translate direct personal experience into positive artistic expressions. This promotes a child's self-esteem and sense of productive accomplishment.

Another positive outcome of art education is that it enables young people to perceive the beauty that surrounds them. We sometimes take our ability to appreciate the visual world for granted. Yet we should not because the ability to perceive is a learned capacity and must be consciously developed. The Inuits living in Alaska, for example, do not have a generic word for *snow*. Instead, they have a particular word or phrase for each kind of snow that they might encounter, for example, wind blown dry snow, or light fluffy snow with fat flakes. They are able to perceive different kinds of snow because they have learned to identify things of importance in the environment. In a similar way, children must learn a visual language that will enable them to perceive beauty in their world. The "beauty" they see lies in their capacity for perception.

It is possible to teach children about art without requiring them to actually make it. But that approach does not provide as much educational impact as one that links values, ideas, and experience. As the old adage tells us "what I hear, I hear; what I see, I remember; what I do, I understand." As we will see shortly, current approaches to art education integrate a range of art-related ideas with the art-making process.

Community-based Goals

Art education makes an impact not only on the developmental potential of the individual, but also on the capacity of individuals to live with one another in a social context. Developing a language and appreciation for art helps establish the foundation for a shared culture. This is especially true for those people who desire to understand their ties to specific cultural communities, but it is also true with regard to our need for integrative links between those diverse communities.

The integrative and community-making potential of art education exists, in part, because of the symbolic nature of art. Images convey meanings that either bring people together or pull them apart. Art education can help create community ties because it paves the way for an understanding of symbolic communication through art. The increased public visibility of fine art and applied art images makes this an increasingly important role for art and art education. Thus, a primary goal of art education in relationship to the community is to develop literacy in the arts. The growing public role of art means that more and more people will be exposed to it and will need to be able to evaluate its various meanings.

Teaching Art

The general educational objectives related to the individual and the community can be achieved by teaching children specific knowledge, skills, and information about art. To do that, children are taught how to make art and, in so doing, how to understand it. Art education gives students the opportunity to explore the specific content of various art disciplines, such as drawing, painting, printmaking, and photography. By making art, students not only develop a greater understanding of what art is, but they also prepare themselves for the possibility of more advanced art making.

This means that there must be specific curriculum-based art programs. One approach to art curriculum has been developed by the Getty Center for Education in the Arts. The Getty Center has developed what it calls a discipline-based art education program (DBAE). It is based on the simple idea that art has content and can be taught. The DBAE curriculum emphasizes four areas: making art, art history, aesthetics, and art criticism. With this kind of curriculum, the ideas the students learn about art are fused with the physical skills of making art. This or any other kind of art curriculum needs to be taught in a sequential and developmental way. Children cannot be introduced to educational material that they are not ready to handle.

A well-developed art education curriculum for students at any age level in the public school system should be rich in content and should provide the art teacher with a useful guide for classroom teaching. With this kind of program, an art teacher can focus on visual elements of art—space, light, color, line, form or shape, and texture. These elements should be part of a teaching strategy that includes experiences of making art inside the classroom that would reveal the meaning of various aspects of art, classroom discussion of each of those elements based on examples from other periods of history or cultures from around the world, and homework assignments involving independent art projects. The specific content of the art curriculum always needs to be tailored to the developmental level of specific age groups.

To teach art adequately, teachers must have more than a conceptual understanding of art. Teachers must also be artists. That means that they must be educational specialists who understand the basic methods, materials, and concepts of their particular disciplines. In many schools, art teachers bring their expertise into a separate art classroom where children learn art. Not only do art teachers need to be artists and to understand art, they also need to have a variety of other knowledge and skills. In particular, they need to have good language skills and must be able to communicate well with children.

Getting a Start

Undergraduate programs require that art education majors do student teaching in a public school system. The teaching experience typically takes place in a high school during a student's senior year. If the student does well, he or she will probably be given first preference when a job becomes available in that school system. There is an advantage to hiring such a person from the point of view of the school system. The individual who has done a good job as a student teacher will already have demonstrated an ability to work successfully as an art teacher. Individuals are also recommended for positions through professional networks that exist between school systems and various art education programs in art colleges and universities.

There was a time when art teachers were paid less than individuals who taught other kinds of subjects. This is no longer true. Laws have been passed that require pay equity between the different academic disciplines in public school systems. That means that salaries begin at a relatively high level. An art education teacher may expect to start at around $24,000 to $26,000 a year. There may be significant variations in salary level depending on the region of the country.

TEACHING ART IN COLLEGE

Art programs in higher education play essentially two roles. First, they are often included as part of the general education requirements that all students in a particular college or university must take. These requirements give students the opportunity to take college-level studio art courses. The objectives of these courses are similar to those in the public school system—they enrich the individual, and provide an opportunity for a hands-on experience in cultural production. These courses are very limited in scope; for the most part, they provide an introductory-level curriculum. Second, art programs can provide a major area of academic concentration for students who wish to study art in depth. There are a variety of such programs and they will be covered in depth in Chapter 8.

The faculty that teach in these programs work on either a full-time or part-time basis. Each has a particular role to play in the educational life of the college or university. They also have a particular meaning in the professional lives of artists who teach. Together, full-time and part-time faculty constitute the backbone of the teaching profession in higher education.

Part-Time Teaching

Part-time or adjunct teaching plays a vital role in higher education that can be a source of significant benefit for the individual teacher and the institution. Many adjunct faculty members choose to teach part-time because they have busy professional lives that take up much of their time and attention. This is especially true for faculty who teach a professional area in which they have expertise as practitioners. Many doctors, lawyers, and businesspeople, for example, not only practice their professions but also teach in colleges or universities on a part-time basis. In fact, this is one of the characteristics of professional education in general. The faculty teach subjects that are directly related to their professional practices. This is true for artists in all of the fine art and applied arts areas.

This situation is advantageous for some artists. That is especially true for artists who are at an early phase of their professional lives, or who have successful careers as fine artists or free-lance artists. The people may be too busy getting their careers off the ground, or they may be too busy with their lucrative professional work to want more than one or two courses to teach at a time. Teaching in college on a part-time basis enables them to supplement their income, spend time sharing their knowledge with students, and derive whatever prestige may be gained from working as a college teacher. Thus, for some artists, teaching on a part-time basis permits them to combine the best of academic and professional life.

Part-time faculty can enliven the learning experiences for students because they often bring the most current and interesting professional issues into the classroom. In that way, students are kept abreast of the latest artistic trends, technical developments, and professional concerns. This is particularly important in the applied arts areas where changes that happen in the practice of the profession can have a direct impact on what students need to know. But the same kind of benefits are made possible by adjunct faculty who teach fine art. These individuals are not only able to add fresh insight into the creative process, but can also serve as positive role models who can provide practical advice about a wide range of professional issues.

Adjunct teaching is not without problems, however. Those individuals who want to teach on a full-time basis may find part-time teaching to be a source of frustration. Adjunct faculty may make $2,000 or more for each course they teach, but they usually do not receive additional benefits such as insurance and retirement programs. In addition, some full-time faculty members in an art college or university may view adjunct faculty as outsiders whose involvement in the education of students should be limited. But despite these difficulties, part-time faculty make a positive contribution and will continue to play a significant role in higher education for many years.

Full-Time Teaching

Full-time college teaching is an especially attractive career option for artists. The pay for full-time faculty is good, though not enough to make a person wealthy. Starting salaries may range from $25,000 to $30,000 per year. In addition, the hours, benefits, and working conditions are highly desirable. An especially attractive aspect of college teaching is that fine and applied artists may continue to pursue professional work for which they can earn additional income. In fact, they are encouraged to do so. Thus, it is possible for art teachers to add many thousands of dollars to their annual income. Moreover, the more professional work they do, the better it is for their academic careers. Being professionally active will help art faculty to be promoted, earn merit salary increases, and receive tenure or guaranteed job security.

Art faculty spend only a few hours each week in the classroom. Depending on the particular institution, they may teach anywhere from twelve to eighteen hours per week. There are, however, additional obligations. Faculty are required to meet with students, evaluate student work, serve on committees, attend meetings, and participate in other college activities. Even with all of these responsibilities, however, full-time art faculty spend far less time working at their primary jobs than individuals in other professional fields. It is also true that faculty in higher education have a great deal of vacation time. They typically have three or four weeks off at Christmas (in between the fall and spring semesters), one week off in the spring and at least three months off in the summer.

An additional benefit is that faculty are eligible to go on sabbatical about every six years. Sabbaticals enable faculty to be paid for time they take off from teaching. A sabbatical will usually last either a half year at full pay, or a full year at half pay. The idea is that faculty need time to get away from teaching to pursue their own professional interests.

Those interests can then be brought back into the classroom to enrich the content and process of teaching.

Academic and professional achievement is rewarded through a system of promotions that includes the ranks of assistant professor, associate professor, and full professor. Criteria for promotion to each rank will differ between schools, but will typically include specified years of teaching experience, professional development such as gallery exhibits, and service to the school. Each promotion carries with it increased prestige and usually a salary increase as well. By the time faculty have achieved the rank of full professor, they should be earning $45,000 to $60,000 a year or more from teaching salary alone.

ART THERAPY

Art therapists do not make art themselves as part of the practice of the profession. Rather they provide a therapeutic service by enabling others to make art. Nonetheless, art therapists must be trained as artists. Their background must include a thorough and practical understanding of how people experience the creative process. This understanding is essential in helping others utilize art making as a medium for self-exploration.

As a profession, art therapy offers interesting choices in relationship to other career options in art. Although practitioners must grapple with issues that lie at the heart of art making—issues such as the personal significance of creativity and the expressive nature of art—they must pursue their own creative impulses in their leisure time. This will not be a satisfying situation for everyone. Art therapy will be frustrating for those individuals who feel as though the core of their professional lives must revolve around actually making art. On the other hand, art therapy offers occupational stability, a clearly defined set of employment possibilities as well as a good salary and benefits.

A Human Service Profession

Art therapy is part of a larger complex of interrelated professions that are dedicated to helping people who have different kinds of problems. Therapeutic teams work in such settings as substance abuse clinics, alcoholism treatment programs, veterans administration hospitals, general hospitals, shelters for battered women, child-life support programs in hospitals, community centers for the elderly, nursing homes, prisons, schools, and psychiatric hospitals. The broad range of clients, patients, and inmates served by these institutions suggests how versatile the healing potential of art therapy can be.

Determining which particular professions should be represented on a therapeutic team will depend on the institutional context in which clients or patients are served. Psychiatric hospitals, nursing homes, and prisons will have different client or inmate populations. Each population will have particular needs that can be best addressed by appropriate human service professionals. Depending on the institutional setting, art therapists may work with doctors, nurses, psychiatrists, psychiatric nurses, mental health workers, psychologists, psychiatric social workers, physical therapists, and/or corrections officers. In addition, each one of these may specialize in the particular problems of the clients they serve. Thus, a psychiatric social worker, along with an art therapist, may have expertise in drug-related problems, geriatric problems, or problems related to children in general hospitals who are receiving treatment for serious medical conditions.

An important aspect of art therapy is that it can serve a number of interrelated goals. The quality of the art produced by patients, however, is not necessarily one of them. The real value of art therapy is that it can be used to diagnose emotional problems, it can be used as part of a treatment plan to resolve those problems, and it can be used to assess the patient's progress during treatment.

The Therapeutic Rationale

The assumption that lies behind art therapy is that the creative art-making process can serve diagnostic and therapeutic goals. At the center of both of these goals is an extremely important idea related to the ground-breaking theories of the psychiatrist Sigmund Freud. He believed that some experiences and resulting emotions can be so unpleasant that our conscious mind will be unable to acknowledge them. Thus, prior experiences may be so difficult to deal with on the conscious level that we may be unaware of their effect on us. These experiences become repressed and are pushed into what Freud called the "unconscious" mind.

Diagnosis

Art therapy tries to address the difficulties that people experience because of their repressed thoughts and feelings. The creative experience is believed to be so spontaneous and to come from such a deep-seated source in our consciousness that it allows repressed feelings and experiences to reach a level of conscious awareness. As a result, art therapy can play an important role in diagnosing emotional problems because it enables the underlying source of problems to be revealed through art.

Imagine, for example, a young child is bothered by problems in her family. When asked about why she is unhappy, she may not be able to identify the source of her feelings. But when asked to draw a picture of her family, she may unintentionally leave one of her parents out of the drawing. This may provide a diagnostic clue that the difficulty lies with that parent. The drawing that springs from a deep and spontaneous source in her mind may allow her repressed feelings to be unintentionally revealed through the images she has produced.

This does not mean that any picture with a family member missing is necessarily an indication of a problem. Nor does it imply that all art can be analyzed for hidden meanings. The point is rather to show the kind of thinking that lies behind art therapy. Art therapy enables patients to express themselves freely and therefore can be useful as part of the diagnostic phase of the therapeutic process. Once the repressed emotion is revealed, it can be the focus of therapeutic intervention.

Art therapy can be useful as an expressive outlet for adults in the same way. Some adults, especially those who are fairly well educated and articulate, are able to use their language ability as a way to maintain a certain kind of emotional distance from other people. They may be very good at discussing professional issues or world politics on an intellectual level, but they may not be as open or as insightful about their own emotional lives. Intelligence by itself does not bring repressed thoughts and feelings into full consciousness. Again, art therapy can be a helpful means for revealing the unconscious mind.

Treatment

Actually, diagnosis is only one part of art therapy. Art therapy can also be used as part of a therapeutic treatment plan for patients. The art-making process not only allows patients to gain insight into repressed thoughts and feelings, it can also provide them with positive experiences that can have therapeutic value. These positive experiences can be a valuable part of a patient's treatment and recovery.

Exactly what those positive experiences might be and what their value is to the patient will depend upon several factors. Those factors include the particular problem a patient might have, the kind of therapeutic approaches that are believed to be helpful, and the particular way in which art making can contribute to the recommended treatment plan. In general terms, the creative experience can achieve therapeutic results because it can help develop a patient's self-esteem, encourage a patient's sense of reality through figurative image making, and provide patients with a record of their therapeutic progress as it is revealed through the art they make. The issue of self-esteem is especially important. In a culture that sometimes seems to place too much emphasis on the surface characteristics of people, art therapy helps give the person a solid core of positive experience.

Treatment is also facilitated when patients see the visual evidence of their own previously unrecognized problems. Patients sometimes resist the interpretations that others make of their thoughts and feelings. But those interpretations can be supported when patients actually see visible indications of what other people are able to detect.

There are other treatment objectives that are related to the fact that art therapy often takes place in groups within various kinds of institutional settings. These group experiences involve artistic assignments that patients may work on together or by themselves. Because creative activity takes place in groups, a large variety of demands are made on patients' interpersonal skills. Patients are encouraged to communicate ideas, share materials and work space, respect the rights of other patients, and accept the institutional rules related to a variety of kinds of social behavior. If they are unable to do so, therapy can provide a focal point for resolving difficulties related to relationships with other people.

These may seem like very simple and ordinary aspects of interacting with people in a group setting. And so they may be for people who do not have serious emotional, physical, or behavioral problems. But they are not so easy for people who do have these problems. These social skills may also be especially difficult when they involve the highly personal and private act of making art in a social setting. The special value of art therapy is that it provides patients with an opportunity to resolve the problems related to bridging the gap between an intense self-preoccupation and the needs of others.

Assessment

The artwork that a patient does can provide information about how a patient is responding to treatment. A patient, for example, may claim to be feeling much better, but may continue to draw pictures of violence, death, or some other themes that have been associated with an underlying emotional or behavioral problem. This means that art therapy is a valuable assessment tool which can reveal significant differences between what patients say and what they may actually be thinking or feeling.

The Therapeutic Alliance

One of the satisfying aspects of the profession is the close bond that can develop between the art therapist and the patient. In fact, their relationship must be based on a high level of mutual trust and respect. One significant potential source of trust that a patient may feel toward a therapist stems from the fact that the therapist is also an artist. This trust is developed because the practitioner believes in the value of art therapy. The therapist's belief in art therapy derives from the therapist having actually experienced the therapeutic effects of art making.

The shared experience of the art-making experience forms an important basis for the trusting communication that takes place between patients and therapists. Trusting communication helps the patient and therapist discuss the possible symbolic significance of the images that are produced. This means that language skills also play a significant role in what the art therapist does. Art therapists use their verbal ability to help patients sift through the veil of emotional entanglements and then to discover the value of their own creativity.

The Therapeutic Team

It is important to stress that the art therapist is one part of a therapeutic team. In an institutional setting there are several different human service professionals who are responsible for the treatment and rehabilitation of patients. Each team member adds some specialized expertise to the patient's care. Doctors, psychiatrists, psychologist, nurses, and art therapists must work together to provide as many opportunities for therapeutic diagnosis and intervention in as many areas of a patient's life as possible.

To do that they work together to develop a treatment plan that provides an approach to therapy that is designed to address the particular recovery needs of a patient. Typically, members of a therapeutic team will meet two or three times each week to discuss the progress of the patient. The members of the team will report on their efforts to help the patient, and on the ways in which the patient has responded to those efforts. Based on those meetings, adjustments in the treatment plan can be formulated. Thus, each member of the therapeutic team serves as a valuable part of the coordinated effort to provide patient care.

The American Art Therapy Association

The American Art Therapy Association (AATA) has played a major role in shaping the professional and educational requirements of the field. It has been active in defining standards for professional practice and ethical conduct as well as guidelines for education and research. Its educational guidelines are especially important and serve as a basis for the professionalization of the field.

Although it is possible to practice the profession with an undergraduate degree in art therapy, the AATA recommends the Master's degree as the entry level requirement for the profession. Educational programs are offered at both the graduate and undergraduate level. Those who wish to pursue the profession should be willing to complete both levels of training. Additional information concerning art therapy may be obtained by writing to The American Art Therapy Association, 1202 Allanson Road, Mundelein, Illinois 60060.

CHAPTER 8

THE EDUCATION OF ARTISTS

Many individuals have their first experience with art in grammar school. In these early grades, art projects are often part of the normal classroom curriculum. At the high school level, separate classes in art are also available. Most school systems with a sufficient budget will make some provision for art instruction. These early encounters with art are important. They can expose young people to the creative process and introduce them to the pleasures of making art. Moreover, developing the ability to produce satisfying art can enable individuals to view themselves in new and positive ways. This can also form the basis for further training in art.

Another significant early experience with art can come from family members and relatives who stimulate and encourage creative activity in children. Many artists come from families with some kind of background in creativity. It is not altogether clear, however, whether those creative influences are genetic or learned. However they are acquired, these influences enable people to develop the visual sensitivity and the eye-hand coordination that is necessary for making art.

PRIVATE ART INSTRUCTION

Almost every community will have some kind of organization that provides art classes for young people and adults. Art classes are sponsored by church groups, community centers, civic organizations, and the YMCA. In addition, there are individuals who hold private art classes in their homes. Individualized private instruction has the advantage of providing students with more personal attention that they sometimes receive in other settings. These classes make art fun and can begin the life-long process of making art.

In addition, there are a variety of art centers that specialize in different levels of instruction. Some art centers include a broad curriculum of art and craft courses that are recreational in nature. Most of these art centers will have basic and intermediate drawing classes. These courses can be useful as a way to learn the fundamental drawing skills that are so valuable as a preparation for more advanced art training at the college level. Art centers offer a wide range of courses for children, teens, and adults. In addition to basic drawing and painting, art centers may offer courses on such diverse subjects as photography, calligraphy, cartooning, comic book art, jewelry design, papermaking, woodcarving, origami (Japanese paper folding), ceramics, silk painting, weaving, and interior decorating.

There are also residential art centers that are designed for more advanced students who are already involved with art as a career. These advanced training centers offer courses in drawing, painting and sculpture by well-known artists. Such courses are typically taught as part of an on-campus program that includes accommodations and meals. These programs allow students to pursue intensive individualized studio work with distinguished professionals.

CREDIT AND NONCREDIT COLLEGE CLASSES

Art instruction is also available through the community education division of art colleges and universities. Classes in drawing, painting, sculpture, and photography, as well as illustration, graphic design, advertising design, and interior design are available in the evening and on the weekend. These classes are usually taught by experienced artists and designers and can provide a serious introduction to a particular kind of art and design. If you want to get the feel of what rigorous art training is like, these classes can help. Some colleges offer a more advanced level of training for individuals who are already working in a professional art or design field.

Although the courses are offered through a college or university, they may or may not be credit classes. Classes for credit meet for a certain number of hours during a semester and can be counted as college courses should an individual decide to apply as a full-time student at an art college or university. Noncredit classes usually meet for a fewer number of hours and cannot be transferred into a college degree program.

ART COLLEGE AND UNIVERSITY PROGRAMS

There is a fairly specific range of art programs that is available in art colleges and universities. The programs that are most often available include drawing, painting, sculpture, printmaking, photography, architecture, computer art, film, video, industrial design, illustration, glass, ceramics, and fiber. In addition, there are more specialized programs including toy design, textile design, cartooning, yacht design, landscape architecture, and book art.

While these provide the range of programs available, they do not exhaust the specialized areas of study within the programs. These programs will usually be taught by faculty who have expertise within a particular field. Their expertise will give students access to unique educational opportunities. There are also interdisciplinary options that allow students to formulate specialized curricula that are tailored to their own interests.

Various kinds of art programs are taught at some forty private art colleges and at hundreds of universities and liberal arts colleges around the country. There are significant educational differences between art colleges and art programs in other institutional settings. There are also significant differences between the basic kinds of degree programs they offer. The first and most important distinction is that which exists between a bachelor of arts (B.A.) degree in art, and a bachelor of fine arts (B.F.A.) degree.

The B.A. degree is not regarded as professional preparation for a career. This is because of the limited number of studio art courses that students are required to take for the degree. Programs of this kind usually do not provide a sufficient amount of technical and conceptual training to enable graduates to work as professional artists or designers. Students who receive the B.A. degree in art are typically required to take approximately one-third of their courses in art, which usually means around fourteen or fifteen studio courses. These degree programs either provide students with a hands-on art appreciation experience, or they provide a means for individualized creative growth, but they do not constitute adequate professional training. Such programs, however, can provide a good introduction to art, and can also serve as a good foundation for graduate-level training.

The B.F.A. degree is regarded as the undergraduate professional degree in art. Programs that offer the B.F.A. degree usually require as many as seventy-two to seventy-eight credit hours or more. This translates into as many as twenty-five studio art courses, which is considerably larger than the number of courses required in B.A. degree programs in art. While a number of artists go on to get a master of fine arts (M.F.A.) degree for advanced art training, the B.F.A. is sometimes the only degree both fine and applied artists will receive. Today, however, the M.F.A. degree is becoming more and more common for professional artists and designers.

Another important consideration in choosing a degree program is whether it is offered in an independent art college, or in a liberal arts college or university. As with degree programs, the institutional setting can make a big difference in a student's education. An art program within a liberal arts college or university will be one among many different kinds of degree programs, including business, engineering, nursing, or liberal arts. The independent art college, by contrast, will have art as its primary educational focus.

There are advantages to both settings. On the one hand, an art program that is part of a larger institution may be desirable for individuals who wish to have a more conventional educational experience and who find curricular diversity and involvement in campus life appealing. On the other hand, those who wish a more specialized educational setting whose energies and resources are devoted primarily to art may feel more at home in an independent art college.

Some art colleges, the Atlanta College of Art or the Minneapolis College of Art and Design, as examples, use the term *college* in the name of the institution. Some schools, however, do not. In fact, there are many excellent art colleges granting the bachelor of fine arts degree that do not make and explicit reference to their degree-granting status in the title of their institution. Examples of such institutions would be the School of Visual Arts (New York), School of the Art Institute of Chicago, Rhode Island School of Design, Kansas City Art Institute, or the California School of Art and Design. Some of these schools grant the master of fine arts degree as well. Anyone interested in learning the degree-granting status of an institution should read the school's catalog closely. The catalog will provide information about degrees and academic programs.

CHOOSING AN ART SCHOOL

There are many colleges and universities to choose from. The key to selecting the right institution is getting as much information as you can. High school guidance counselors and art teachers will have printed information about art schools. Seeking their help and guidance can provide a good starting point as you begin to determine which school is right for you. Another useful resource for basic information on art colleges and art programs in liberal art colleges and universities is the *Guide to American Art Schools* by John D. Werenko. In addition, many institutions will send a representative to high schools to talk about their schools and answer students' questions. Check your high school bulletin board or ask your guidance counselor about these visitations.

Based on the preliminary information you obtain from these sources, make a list of those schools that interest you. If you write or call a school's admissions office, they will send you a catalog that describes their basic educational mission, the school's curriculum (the areas of study they offer), the degrees they offer, as well as the background of their faculty members. General information will usually be provided about students, as well as more specific information about facilities. The catalog will also provide information about the school's tuition and fees, and also their admissions procedures.

Another excellent source of information is the National Portfolio Day. This is actually a series of events during which a large number of art school representatives gather in one place to meet with students, review their portfolios, and answer questions. There are about twenty-five to thirty portfolio-day events each year, which are accessible to students in every part of the country. Your high school art teacher or guidance counselor will have information about dates and locations for the National Portfolio Day nearest you.

The institutions that participate in the National Portfolio Day are all members of the National Association of Schools of Art and Design (NASAD). This association accredits art and design programs in colleges and universities and helps to insure a high level of academic quality among participating institutions. Information about NASAD and the schools that it accredits are available by writing to the National Association of Schools of Art and Design, 11250 Roger Bacon Drive, Suite 21, Reston, VA 22090.

The National Association of College Admission Counselors sponsors the National College Fair, which can also provide valuable information about art colleges and universities. There are about thirty-five of these fairs around the country. You can obtain information about the fairs by talking to your guidance counselor, or writing to the National Association of College Admissions Counselors, Suite 430, 1800 Diagonal Road, Alexandria, VA 22314.

Once you have narrowed your choice of schools down to a manageable number, you should plan a visit to each one of them. This may seem like a large task, but you are making an important decision and should find out as much about each school as you can. More than one student has found a college catalog appealing only to be disappointed once they have spent some time on campus.

It is not necessary to have a clear idea about exactly what art area you want to study in college. Some schools will encourage students to indicate a basic area of interest when they apply, or to select a basic area of study when they register for classes. But many schools do not. They know that students who are applying to an art school may not have enough information to choose a particular area of study. These schools often will provide a foundation-level curriculum in the freshman year, which enables students to have the opportunity of becoming exposed to various art disciplines, media, and art-making processes before they concentrate on one area. It is also not uncommon for students to change their majors more than once while they are in college.

GETTING INTO AN ART COLLEGE

There are many primary factors that contribute to getting into art school that are ostensibly of equal significance, but in reality can have variable impact on an admission decision. The three factors are high school grades (art grades as well as academic grades), the Scholastic Aptitude Test (SAT) score, and the portfolio of art work. For students who are transferring from another college (either another art college, a community college, a liberal arts college, or a university), college grades would be considered. Students who apply from a foreign country other than Canada or another English-speaking country will also have to score adequately on a standardized language test, such as the Test of English as a Foreign Language (TOEFL).

The significance of these grades, test scores, and portfolio will vary if there is a noticeable difference between them. A student with an average portfolio and excellent grades will have a better chance of being accepted than a student with an average portfolio and weak grades. Similarly, a student with a strong portfolio and good grades will have a better chance than one who has a strong portfolio and weak grades.

The portfolio is the one part of the admission process that separates art students from those students who are seeking admission to other kinds of college programs. A portfolio should include the art or design work that a student wants to have considered by the admissions committee. A school will typically want to see twelve to fifteen pieces of work in a portfolio. Regardless of the art area in which one would like to specialize in college, perhaps the single most important works to include in the portfolio are life drawings.

A student who plans on applying to art college should take at least one basic drawing course and then draw from life as much as possible. Drawings that are copies of other drawings or photographs are not of much value. The best life drawings and paintings should be included in a portfolio. Other artwork may be required by the particular college admissions requirements and may include photographs or drafting depending on the kind of program to which one is applying. Each school will publish its admission requirements in the catalog. Admission requirements and other information may be obtained by calling or writing to the school's admission office. There are also some general guides to the admissions process. Three useful books are *How to Get Into College* by Clifford J. Caine; *Your College Application* by Scott Gelband, Catherine Kubale, and Eric Schorr; and *A Student's Guide to College Admissions* by Harlow Unger.

SCHOLARSHIPS AND LOANS

The cost of an art education can be considerable. Fortunately there are many grants, loans, scholarships, work-study programs, and payment plans to help pay for education. Grants are an especially good source of funds because the money is typically based on a student's financial need and does not have to be paid back. The federal government has established Pell Grants which provide money directly to individual students. There are also Supplemental Educational Opportunity Grants that are available for students who demonstrate exceptional financial need. In addition, states provide a variety of grants that may be used in addition to the federal grants.

Campus-based funding sources involve federal money that is funneled to students through colleges and universities. The Perkins Loan Program, for example, provides money to schools, which in turn loan money directly to their students. The Supplemental Educational Opportunity Grant is another federal funding source that is available to colleges and universities which they pass on to students.

Many students take out loans for college through banks, credit unions, or savings and loan institutions. The Stanford Student Loan (formerly the Guaranteed Student Loan) is one of the most frequently used programs. The Supplemental Loan for Students provides additional loan money for students who are deemed financially independent of their parents. In addition, parents of college students may take out educational loans for their children through the Parent Loans for Undergraduate Students (PLUS) program.

Scholarships provide direct aid to students and come from a wide range of institutional sources. The National Merit Scholarship is a major source of money that comes from the National Merit Scholarship Corporation. Scholarships are also provided by a variety of state government programs and local civic groups, as well as private and religious organizations. Like grants, scholarships do not have to be repaid. Unlike grants, however, they are typically awarded to students with a record of high academic achievement. Most colleges and universities will also make scholarship money available to their own students.

Beyond these sources, colleges have a variety of financial plans for students including installment payments, prepayment plans, and work-study options. Colleges and universities understand the burden of paying for an education and have many ways to help ease the load. Prospective students should consult the financial aid office at the college of their choice. In addition, there are publications that can provide good information about college costs and financial aid: *Paying For College* by Gerald Krefetz, *The College Cost Book* published by College Board Publications, and *The College Blue Book: Scholarships, Fellowships, Grants and Loans* published by the Macmillan Publishing Company.

B.F.A. DEGREE PROGRAMS

A bachelor of fine arts degree program, like other undergraduate degree programs, takes four years to complete. It typically begins with a foundation curriculum in the first year. A foundation curriculum is usually required of all students in a particular school and might typically include a drawing course, a design course of some kind, perhaps an elective studio course, as well as a writing and literature course. Some schools have a greater range of foundation programs, depending on the student's major, which may include more specialized studio courses and liberal arts courses. By the time students enter their second year, they will usually have selected a major in one of the art or design areas if they have not already done so in the first year. Some schools also allow students to pursue an individualized curriculum that is usually interdisciplinary in nature and integrates the subject matter of more than one art or design discipline.

The "major" is an area of academic concentration in one of the art or design disciplines. It enables students to specialize in such studio areas as drawing, painting, sculpture, printmaking, photography, illustration, graphic design, or advertising design. The curriculum within each department addresses a full range of technical, aesthetic, and professional issues. Courses are taken in a loosely structured sequence that increases the students' exposure to what they need to learn. By the time students have entered their last year, they work much more independently than is the case in their first two years. By the senior year, the student's work is expected to be at or near a basic professional level.

The heart of a degree program is the studio art courses. But there is another area in the curriculum that should be emphasized as well. This area involves the general range of liberal arts courses that all students in all B.F.A. degree programs are required to take. Students must take about one-third of their course work in such areas as literature, history, philosophy, psychology, sociology, economics, mathematics, and science. Students who complete the degree program are expected to read and write with a degree of proficiency that will enable them to fulfill their considerable need for professional-level communications.

The particular curriculum at art colleges and universities will vary not only in terms of the various art areas taught, but also in terms of the structure of each program. For example, not all schools offer interior design or art education. In addition, at some schools the four basic fine arts areas may be a part of what is called the "fine arts" major, while at other schools each area constitutes a separate major. In either case, the content of particular areas of study are fairly similar between schools.

Drawing

The term *drawing* is widely used and can refer to everything from technical drafting to loose sketching. When the term is used to describe a particular approach to making fine art, the term becomes even more ambiguous. That is because a variety of media may be used to create an art product that can take on a number of different looks. Some drawings look like what one might typically think of as a pencil or ink drawing, but those that are produced with crayons, charcoal, computers, paint, or some combination of these media may not. In fact, a college drawing program is likely to include a course that explores the basic question, "What is a drawing?" There are many answers.

To get to those answers, however, students start out with the basics. Most schools continue to emphasize figure drawing as the foundation not only of drawing as a discipline, but also of other art areas as well. Beyond learning the basic techniques of line and shading used for rendering, students develop more individual approaches to expression through drawing. Courses evolve in a progressive fashion from fundamentals to more advanced problems to personal aesthetic goals.

Drawing is not offered as a major or area of concentration in all art schools. One reason for that is because drawing is sometimes regarded as a means to an end rather than an end in itself. Thus, it can be used to sketch out ideas on paper for paintings, sculpture, or printmaking. Another reason, is that drawing is used as the basic medium for illustration, which is often emphasized in the curriculum rather than the process used to achieve it.

When there is a focus on drawing as an end in itself, the results bring the artists and the viewer in touch with the oldest and most direct of the various art media. Drawing predates writing as a form of personal expression and communication. Drawing is also perhaps the most portable of all media. Artists sketch endlessly wherever they go. There is an immediacy and authenticity about it that many artists enjoy. Once a mark is set on paper, it is a permanent record of an artist's impulse or intention. For that reason, drawing has an honesty and purity about it that has been the foundation of all art making for centuries.

Painting

There was a time when it was easy to identify painting. Paintings were made with oil paint or some other paint medium that was applied to the two-dimensional surface of a square canvas. Many paintings are still made that way. Today, however, work that is classified as painting is not at all limited by those constraints. Painting is done with anything that will stick to a surface that may or may not be two-dimensional. In fact, the boundaries of painting and sculpture are sometimes blurred because the application of surface color is becoming more accepted in sculpture and because painting has sought a variety of three-dimensional surfaces.

Students learn how to manipulate paint as a physical medium. The various paints they learn how to use include oil, acrylic, egg tempera, and encaustic (melted wax mixed with pigment). They also learn how to build stretchers (the frame on which canvas is hung), to stretch and fix canvas on frames, and to prepare the canvas with gesso or other substances so that paint will properly adhere to its surface.

Learning how to paint involves developing the use of technique as a means to solving personally formulated aesthetic problems. At the basic level, students develop their skills through the study of color, space, shape, form, texture, and surface. In addition, most art schools begin with a focus on traditional subjects such as the figure, still life, and landscapes. At the more advanced level, students will work independently and are encouraged to explore their own ideas.

Sculpture

As with other fine art areas, sculpture has a long tradition of materials and methods but is currently undergoing significant changes. Undergraduate programs in sculpture provide students with the opportunity to become familiar with those traditions. But those programs also enable students to take their work into new areas. Faculty members who have a more traditional orientation to sculpture may resist regarding work made with new materials and methods as sculpture. But no one seems resistant to appreciating good art regardless of what it is made of or what it is called.

Perhaps the one consistent characteristic of sculpture is that it requires the ability to address three-dimensional spatial problems. Students not only learn to think in spatial terms, they also learn the methods and materials required to create three-dimensional forms. Such concepts as shape, form, symmetry, and surface are explored through the techniques and materials of sculpture. The more traditional materials that students use are clay, stone, wood, metal, paper, resin, and fiberglass. But less conventional materials are now becoming common as well. These include tools, household and industrial products, mounds of soil, wire, used tires, street signs, electronic equipment, shopping carts, trash cans, fish tanks, cans of food, glass, plastic, hay, mud, used clothing, and anything else you might be able to imagine.

Printmaking

Printmaking involves course work that focuses heavily on the technologies of the discipline. These technologies include: relief, intaglio, lithography, and screen printing. As with other art-making disciplines, each printmaking methodology is characterized by distinctive kinds of appearance. Printmaking is deeply rooted in the long history of fine art image making, yet has become a standard medium for the even the most avant-guarde aesthetic approaches.

A major part of a printmaker's education involves learning the four basic technologies. Relief printmaking works in the same way that rubber stamps produce images. The process begins by making cuts into the surface of wood or linoleum and then applying ink to the raised surface. Paper is then pressed onto the inked surface and an image appears.

Intaglio is made in the reverse way. Shallow scratches or marks are made on the surface of a copper or steel plate. Ink is rubbed into the marks and then the rest of the ink is wiped off the surface area that has not been scratched or marked. Paper is then pressed onto the metal plate with sufficient force so that it picks up the ink that is held within the marks that have been made in the surface of the plate. Lithography is a somewhat involved process of printing from a flat stone or metal surface on which the image to be printed is ink-receptive and the blank area is ink-repellent. The ink-receptive areas form the image-making surface of the stone or metal surface. Screen printing basically involves a process of stenciling that is done through a fine mesh of fabric.

Photography

Photography programs usually begin with an introduction to the technology of image making. Learning the technology of photography involves familiarity with different kinds of cameras, filters, lenses, film, lighting equipment, as well as various darkroom procedures and techniques. Through these procedures students learn that there is a great deal to photographic image making that happens after the picture is taken. Beyond basic film developing, darkroom techniques include hand mixing and applied emulsions, color separation, solarization, bleaching, toning, and hand coloring. Schools that include electronic imaging with the computer will introduce students to still video cameras, scanners, and the software for image processing.

In addition, most schools will emphasize the differences between studio and location shooting. Within these differences, programs will focus on such specializations as still life, portraiture, architecture and interiors, landscapes, illustration, fashion, travel, news, and photojournalism. Another basic distinction that students are required to learn is the difference between color and black-and-white photography. Beyond the various issues of technique and application is the concern with learning photography as a means of personal expression. This is just as important in the various applied photography uses as it is in fine art photography.

Interior Design

The technical requirements of the field of interior design are demanding and numerous. As a result, undergraduate programs are often highly structured to insure that students will be exposed to all of the course material they need. In addition to a wide variety of technical skills and information, students must become familiar with the design principles, styles, and product lines they will use to create safe, comfortable, and appealing interiors.

Drafting is essential to interior design. As a result, students learn to draw floor plans, elevations, axonometric perspectives, and reflected ceiling plans in order to convey design ideas as well as technical information to contractors and vendors. In addition, they must become familiar with various kinds of building and mechanical systems including heating, ventilation, and air conditioning. Building and fire codes are typically taken into consideration, especially for interiors that serve the public. Courses that focus on such specialty areas as acoustics and lighting are also valuable for interior design students.

In addition, students learn to focus on the client's needs and to build a design concept around those needs. A design concept will define an aesthetic approach for a client. That approach will then form the basis for selecting the colors, fabrics, surface finishes, furniture, and accessories needed to achieve the desired result.

All of these various elements are integrated into a curriculum which focuses on the process of interior design. Students learn how to utilize these elements to satisfy the needs of particular kinds of clients. Interior design programs will typically offer courses that focus on issues and problems related to a variety of kinds of interiors, such as those required for families, professional offices, large corporations, retail stores, theaters, restaurants, schools, and other kinds of institutions.

Advertising Design and Graphic Design

Advertising design is concerned with teaching students technical skills, creative thinking, and problem-solving abilities. The technical skills include all of those methods and materials that are used to actually make the advertisements. Students learn how to use markers, photographs, illustrations, press type, type faces, and other materials to produce advertisements. Drawing skills used in making comps as well as writing skills are taught. There is also a growing emphasis in use of computers to teach advertising design. Computers, however, should be regarded as technical aids to good design and learning how to use them should not be regarded as an educational objective in itself.

The other basic educational goal is creative thinking. Students are taught how to solve the client's basic problem—selling a product. To do that a variety of issues are emphasized, such as how to establish advertising themes, advertising strategies that develop over time, ethical issues, legal questions, social conditions, and demographics. Language skills are emphasized so that students can learn how to make verbal presentations to clients.

The educational goals for graphic design are similar to those in advertising design. The primary difference is in the nature of the final design and the objectives of those designs. Graphic design is used to instruct, inform, or call attention to institutions, products, and ideas. Therefore, students learn the technical and conceptual skills necessary to produce package design, brochures, logos, and environmental design systems. While a broad range of skills should be developed, students are often encouraged to focus on a particular area of interest in preparation for the development of their portfolios.

Illustration

This is a professional discipline that is closely tied to the areas of advertising design and graphic design. Illustration is often a component of the work done in these fields, and is seldom used outside of some kind of design context. These three areas are closely connected on the academic level and are therefore often part of a single department in art colleges or art programs in universities.

There are also obvious and significant differences between these areas. As we saw in Chapter 6, illustration is often similar in general appearance to representational fine art drawing or painting. Students who study illustration are expected to learn basic technical skills using various media including pen and ink, pastel, and paint. An emphasis is placed on teaching students how to use those skills as a means of conveying ideas visually. In addition, students are encouraged to develop a personal style that will set them apart as illustrators.

Computer Art and Graphics

A growing number of schools now offer degree programs in the computer for fine art and design areas. This trend reflects the increasing demand for computer applications in professional situations. However, a special note needs to be added about the role of computers in the education of art students. Some of the most respected art colleges in the country do not offer a separate major in computer art or graphics and have no current plans to do so.

The reason for this may sound a bit contradictory, but it is not: art schools may not have a specific major in computer art and design because the computer has become increasingly important in all of the art and design areas. Many schools that do not offer undergraduate degree programs in computers have excellent computer courses, computer labs, and lab assistants that serve all of the art and design degree programs. Regardless of one's undergraduate major, computers are likely to be an important option for creative production. Students who major in painting, sculpture, photography, graphic design, or interior design, for example, will want to learn how to use a computer to further their professional objectives.

Computer courses, lab facilities, and lab assistants are therefore in place to serve the computer needs of the entire art college community. Another approach to integrating computers into the curriculum is to offer a concentration in computers. For example, a student might major in graphic design with an emphasis in computer-based design. Or a student who is studying interior design may want to have a concentration in computers in order to learn how to do computer-aided drafting and design work.

Whether one majors in computers or learns the computer as part of the larger program of study within a discipline, the approach to learning will be the same. Students learn how to use computer hardware and software. Hardware refers to the various kinds of equipment, including computers, digitizing equipment (e.g., video and flatbed scanners), and laser printers. Software refers to various kinds of programs that are coded instructions that are fed into a computer enabling the computer user to do different kinds of art or design work. There are, for example, paint programs, drawing programs, and graphic design programs. Programs enable artists and designers to do two-dimensional work as well as three-dimensional modeling on the computer.

M.F.A. DEGREE PROGRAMS

Students who enter a master of fine arts degree program are expected to refine their technical skills and develop a personal body of advanced level work. On the undergraduate level, students receive a solid introduction to the techniques and skills of a number of different disciplines. At the undergraduate level, students focus on the skills of a number of different disciplines. At the graduate level, students focus on the skills and techniques of one particular discipline. That focus will typically include mastering conventional material and methods of the discipline, but will also include a deep exploration of experimental approaches to art making.

Graduate school sometimes means that students will shift focus from one area of undergraduate study to a different area in a graduate program. Someone who majored in painting on the undergraduate level, for example, may enter a graduate program to study illustration. Students who enter a graduate program are likely to make many similar changes in discipline. That is important because it provides an additional level of educational flexibility as students discover their real professional interests. Such changes typically necessitate the student to refocus on new technical skills.

The mastery of technical proficiency will serve in the development of a graduate student's personal vision. This vision involves the approach that a student will take in expressing ideas. The individual style that is typically associated with a mature artist is sometimes regarded as a superficial manifestation of the concepts that lie at the heart of artistic creativity. However, this is not quite correct. It is rather the case that style and conceptual content work in an interdependent relationship to convey the full and multifaceted intention of art.

The content of art is important at the graduate level and students often spend a large amount of time engaged in research to strengthen it. Although research can include experimentation with the tools and methods of art making, it can also mean developing a body of knowledge and ideas that support conceptual content. This kind of research involves becoming intimately familiar with art history, as well as with a broad range of liberal arts areas.

CHAPTER 9

INTERNATIONAL ART

Because of efficient transportation and sophisticated communication technology, the world is rapidly becoming a "global village." The increase in various kinds of contacts between countries is having an impact on professional art in two ways. First, there are opportunities in the fine arts for individuals to sell their work in other parts of the world, especially Europe. Second, international trade has created areas of growth in a number of the applied arts as well.

FINE ART

Until as late as the 1940s Europe was the art capital of the world. Up to that time the art community in America looked to Europe for artistic inspiration. Museums and private collectors were therefore primarily concerned with European artists. At the same time, however, an indigenous American art was developing. Finally, with the emergence of abstract expressionism in the 1940s, American art suddenly began to dominate the international scene. That paved the way for a strong market for American art in Europe, and the rest of the world, which has continued over the years.

In practical terms, that means that there is a lively market in Europe for American art. In the United States, the major art markets are limited to cities like New York, Chicago, and Los Angeles. But in Europe, there are several major art centers. These include the cities of Cologne, Düsseldorf, Milan, Rome, Naples, Paris, Amsterdam, and, to some extent, London.

It is important for American artists to show in European galleries for two reasons. First, Europeans have a long tradition of respect and appreciation for fine art, therefore, the art market in Europe is strong because Europeans like to buy art. Therefore, the galleries in Europe provide good opportunities for Americans to sell their art. Second, selling in Europe increases the American artist's reputation back in the United States. Selling art in general increases an artist's reputation because it changes perceptions of the value of the artist's work, but those perceptions can be influenced, in particular, by assumptions that Americans make about the sophisticated tastes of European buyers.

In order to sell work in a European gallery, an artist must first have his or her art seen by a dealer who wants to show it. European gallery dealers must therefore see the artist's work. European gallery dealers come to the United States to look for artists whose work they would like to represent. Most European dealers look for art in New York. They do so in part because New York is closer to Europe than other cities, and also because it has such a high concentration of artists. Artists may live and work anywhere in the United States, but at some point they must show their work in New York. Unless they do, their work may not be discovered because it is unlikely that European gallery dealers will travel to other parts of the United States to see their work.

In addition to having many important galleries and museums, Europe has other very venues for selling art. Group shows, in particular, are a good way for young artists to become established on the continent. The important group shows are only held every two or four years. One group show, Documenta, which takes place in Kassel, Germany, is held every five years and is organized by a different museum curator each time. This is perhaps the most important group show in the world. Artists from the United States are invited to participate. The Venice Biennale is held every two years in Italy. In that group show, each participating country has its own pavilion and presents the work of a select number of artists. The Paris Biennale is also held every two years, and is also an excellent vehicle for young artists because the show is restricted to individuals who are thirty-five years old or younger.

Art fairs are also important in the European art scene. Dealers lease floor space at a fair for one week to sell the work of the artists they represent. The most important of these fairs takes place in Basel, Switzerland, during the month of June. The fair is held in an enormous two-story building which is rented to two hundred art dealers. Cologne and Düsseldorf are sister cities in Germany that also have an important art fair that takes place in October. Other fairs take place in Paris and also in Madrid, Spain.

The art market in Japan has been thriving in recent years. In fact, the market in Japan is superseding that of Europe. The recent record-breaking sale of Van Gogh's *Portrait of Dr. Gachet,* for example, went to a Japanese collector for over $82 million. Other dazzling Japanese sales include Renoir's *Au Moulin De La Galette* for $78 million, and Van Gogh's *Sunflowers* for $54 million. Such purchases, however, are motivated largely by the investment value of works done by well-established artists from the past. But here is an emerging market for the work of living American artists. Like the European market, these sales are almost exclusively arranged by art dealers.

The situation in China presents a considerably different situation than is found in Europe or the United States and therefore provides an instructive comparison. For the most part, individuals in China do not collect art—at least they do not collect expensive art. There is no art market as we know it. Most of the galleries in China are an extension of state-owned and -operated museums. There are a few commercial galleries, but these sell mainly to tourists or to the few large companies that need art for their executive offices.

The most successful fine artists in China are supported by the government. They are hired by a state-owned museum or cultural center and hold staff positions as artists. These artists are given studio space to work, subsidized housing, and a salary that is approximately equal to what a college professor earns. In addition, they may sell their paintings in galleries that are part of the institutions in which they work.

Artists who have not reached that level may teach in art colleges or universities.

The Chinese prefer traditional themes in art. Landscapes are very popular, but subject matter in paintings may also include still life, flowers, and animals. There is relatively little figurative work that depicts people. The style in painting can range from being very naturalistic to fairly abstract. Artists who have been influenced by the Western tradition in art may work with oil paint or acrylic, but the traditional medium of ink and organically derived colors on rice paper is the most frequently used.

These factors mean that there is really not much of an art market in China for American artists. The basic problem is that while Chinese people have a growing interest in the West and in the United States in particular, they do not have much individual wealth with which they can buy art. This is because China is still laboring under a centralized economic system, which means that the state controls nearly all of the economic activity in the country. There is, however, a distinct trend toward private enterprise in China which may allow people to have more money in years to come. Should that develop in any significant way, the art market in China may open up to American artists.

There is one area that does offer possibilities for American artists. The Chinese are interested in learning more about Western art styles and techniques. A growing number of artists are now being invited to lecture and teach in art colleges and universities in China. A variety of cultural exchange programs have enabled American artists to travel to China. In the process, they are not only able to teach but to learn as well.

APPLIED ART

There is some international design, but it is limited by practical considerations. Because of language barriers, it is difficult to create advertising and graphic design in one country for use in another country. There are also important cultural differences to consider. Colors, for example, can have different meaning to people in various cultures.

Also, what is considered to be humorous, romantic, fashionable, or in good taste will often vary from one country to another. Because both graphic design and advertising make use of symbolic communication to convey ideas, linguistic and cultural differences between countries have to be considered in any design project.

For those reasons, international design is more likely to occur when an international company makes use of design talents in the countries in which it wants to sell its products. This is especially true for companies in Japan, China, or Korea that wish to enter American or European markets. Minolta, for example, is a Japanese company that hired an American design firm to create a logo for its line of cameras. That logo was designed to satisfy Western aesthetic sensibilities, and yet it also retains vague references to Japanese culture.

Some design work that is produced for a domestic market becomes international when the company whose product bears a particular logo begins to expand internationally. There are many examples of design that have become international in that way. Logos for Mercedes-Benz, BMW, Coca-Cola, and McDonald's restaurants would be examples. Airlines with international markets also have logos that are widely recognized.

Interior design is also done on the international level. American firms, both large and small, have done projects all over the world. These interior design assignments are often tied to larger architectural projects. Clients may want their interior design projects done by an American company for a variety of reasons, such as the prestige of the design firm, or because the design firm specializes in particular kinds of projects, such as hotels. There are some American firms that have offices overseas, but those offices are largely staffed by local designers. The international design that is important to career opportunities for Americans involves work done in the United States for overseas clients.

While there are certain barriers that limit the opportunities for international interior design, there are design projects being done by American firms in other countries. These projects can be handled without a great deal of difficulty because many aspects of the design process for an overseas project can be done in the United States without an intimate knowledge of the country's language or culture. Schematic design and design development, for example, can be done without a great deal of local knowledge. The knowledge that is required is usually acquired during programming when the client discusses various needs concerning the interior. Cultural issues related to space and the way it is used will be identifiable by the client and then integrated into the design.

There are technical issues that do need to be addressed, however. Projects that are done by a United States design firm for a European client, for example, will make use of technical drawings based on the metric system rather than our system of inches and feet. It is also often necessary for American design firms to work with an indigenous design or architectural firm to handle local regulations, to file construction documents, and to be responsible for the construction administration.

In fashion design, Europe sets the standards and is very involved in the international market. For that reason, the United States has done relatively little exporting. The major exception is in the area of sportswear. Blue jeans, in particular, are the major contribution of America to international fashion design. Jeans are in demand all over the world. In Russia, for example, blue jeans have been a popular black market item. The United States exports other sportswear including hiking books, running shoes, and athletic clothing.

Photography and illustration can be international under certain conditions. A stock agency that we discussed earlier, The Image Bank, has sixty-two offices in countries around the world. A key criterion that this company uses to select the photographers and illustrators is the universality of the images they produce. Because the photographs and illustrations that The Image Bank has in stock are sold by all or most of its offices around the world, the images must have international marketability. That means that images with a distinctly regional flavor may not be suitable for the requirements of international companies. Photographs of roadside diners in Cincinnati, for example, may not be of much value to art directors in Milan, Paris, Sidney, or Tokyo. The best images are those that can be understood and appreciated by people from many countries and cultures.

Free-lance photographers and illustrators who are not represented by stock agencies are also able to work on an international basis. Photography involves an interpretive recording of what already exists. Therefore, a photographer can step into another society and record rather than design reality in a personal way. Similarly, illustration represents an existing reality—it does not create abstract designs that may or may not be fully appreciated.

ART SCHOOLS

Students who wish to study art in another country have many excellent schools to choose from. Those schools are listed in a publication of The Young International Creators' Organization (Young ICO), an international art-school network. In its first annual publication, *Universiart: Worldwide Graduate Artworks,* Young ICO has compiled the best work of students who have graduated from over 100 art schools in thirty-four countries.

This publication is a valuable reference. It lists the names, addresses, and major areas of study of each of the participating institutions. It also presents over one thousand glossy photographs of a full range of student work in all of the fine and applied art areas. *Universiart* provides readers an opportunity to see exactly what level of work is expected of students who graduate from an art college and enter the world of professional art and design. These are excellent examples of professional level work that should inspire students to intensify their education in art. For information on obtaining a copy of *Universiart* write to: Young ICO Headquarters, C/-JCA Press Division, 5-12-3 Higashi-kaigan Kita, Chigasaki, Kanagawa Japan. Their telephone number is 81 (Japan)-467-852725.

Another aspect of the international education of art students needs to be considered as well. There is a growing number of students from all over the world who are coming to the United States to study art and design. This has had a valuable impact on art schools as they discover how students from other countries interpret and express artistic ideas. That educational relationship, however, is reciprocal. Many of the international students who study in the United States return to their native countries, where they produce art and design that will influence future generations. As the educational movement of art students between countries increases over the years, the language and impact of art will become more and more international.

RECOMMENDED READINGS

BOOKS

The books included in the list below describe various aspects of fine and applied art careers in greater detail. These publications should be available at larger public libraries in most cities. The libraries usually belong to an interlibrary loan service so if the book you want is not immediately available, your local library should be able to get it for you.

Abbot, Susan and Barbara Webb. *Fine Art Publicity: The Complete Guide for Galleries and Artists*. Stamford, CT: The Arts Business News Library, 1991.

Brackman, Henrietta. *The Perfect Portfolio: Professional Techniques for Presenting and Selling Your Photographs*. New York: Amphoto, 1984.

Caine, Clifford J. *How to Get Into College: A Step-by-Step Manual*. Lexington, MA: The Stephen Greene Press, 1985.

Caplin, Lee. *The Business of Art,* second edition. Englewood Cliffs, NJ: Prentice-Hall, 1989.

Casewit, Curtis W. *Making a Living in the Fine Arts: Advice from the Pros*. New York: Macmillan Publishing, 1981.

Choosing Design. Minneapolis: The Core of Understanding Book Project, 1991.

Cochrane, Diane. *The Business of Art: A Comprehensive Guide to Business Practices for Artists*. New York: Watson-Guptill Publications, 1988.

Craig, James. *Graphic Design Career Guide*. New York: Watson-Guptill Publications, 1983.

Gold, Ed. *The Business of Graphic Design: A Sensible Approach to Marketing and Managing a Graphic Design Firm*. New York: Watson-Guptill Publications, 1985.

Goodman, Calvin J. *Art Marketing Handbook*. Los Angeles: gee tee bee, 1991.

Green, Laura R., ed. *Money for Artists. A Guide to Grants and Awards for Individual Artists*. New York: American Council for the Arts, 1987.

Heller, Steven and Lita Talarico *Design Career: Practical Knowledge for Beginning Illustrators and Graphic Designers*. New York: Van Nostrand Reinhold Company, 1987.

Holden, Donald. *Art Career Guide*. New York: Watson-Guptill Publications, 1983.

Horenstein, Henry. *The Photographer's Source: A Complete Catalogue*. New York: Simon & Shuster, 1989.

Hoover, Deborah A. *Supporting Yourself as an Artist: A Practical Guide,* second edition. New York: Oxford University Press, 1989.

Ito, Dee. *The School of Visual Arts Guide to Careers*. New York: McGraw-Hill Books, 1987.

Kerlow, Isaac V. and Judson Rosebush. *Computer Graphics for Designers and Artists,* second edition. New York: Van Nostrand Reinhold Co., 1987.

Langley, Stephen and James Abruzzo. *Jobs in Arts and Media Management: What They Are and How to Get One!* New York: American Council for the Arts, 1989.

Marquard, Ed. *Graphic Design Presentations.* New York: Van Nostrand Reinhold Company, 1986.

McCann, Michael. *Health Hazards Manual for Artists.* New York: Lyons & Buford, Publishers, 1985.

Niemeyer, Suzanne, ed. *Money for Visual Artists.* New York: American Council for the Arts, 1991.

The College Blue Book: *Scholarships, Fellowships, Grants and Loans.* New York: Macmillan Publishing, 1985.

Unger, Harlow G. *A Student's Guide to College Admissions.* New York: Facts on File Publications, 1986.

PERIODICALS

Applied Art Publications

Apparel Manufacturing
Forge Associate Publications, Inc.
Riverside, CT 06878

Apparel News South
945 South Wall Street
Los Angeles, CA 90015

Body Fashions
Harcourt Brace Jovanovich, Inc.
757 Third Avenue
New York, NY 11017

California Apparel News
945 South Wall Street
Los Angeles, CA 90015

Chicago Apparel News
350 Orleans
Suite 1045
Chicago, IL 60654

Communication Arts
410 Sherman Avenue
P.O. Box 10300
Palo Alto, CA 94303

Computer Pictures
25550 Hawthorne Boulevard
Suite 314
Torrance, CA 90505

Creation: International Graphic Design, Art, and Illustration
8-4-17 Ginza
Chou-ku, Tokyo 104
Japan

Design: The International Magazine for Designers and Their
Clients
28 Haymarket
London SW1Y 4SU
United Kingdom

Design World: The International Journal of Design
 Design Editorial Pty. Ltd.
 11 School Road, Rerny Creek
 Victoria, 3786
 Australia

Fashion International
 153 East 87th Street
 New York, NY 10128

Graphis: The International Magazine of Design and Communication
 Graphis US, Inc.
 141 Lexington Avenue
 New York, NY 10016

How: The Bottomline Design Magazine
 F & W Publications, Inc.
 1507 Dana Avenue
 Cincinnati, OH 45207

Idea: International Advertising Art
 Siebundo Shinkosha Publishing Co., Ltd.
 1-13-7 Yoyoicho, Nakanoku
 Tokyo, 164
 Japan

Identity
 ST Publications, Inc.
 407 Gilbert Avenue
 Cincinnati, OH 45020

Ink & Gall
 Box 1469
 Taos, NM 87571

Interior Design
249 W. 17th Street
New York, NY 10011

Interiors
Box 1993
Marion, OH 43405-1933

MacWorld
501 Second Street
San Francisco, CA 94107

novum gebrauchsgraphic
Beuckmann Muchen
D-8000 Muchen 2
Germany

Print
RC Publications, Inc.
3200 Tower Oaks Boulevard
Rockville, MD 20852

Sportswear International
29 West 38th Street
New York, NY 10003

Step-By-Step Graphics
Step-by-Step Publishing
Dynamic Graphics, Inc.
6000 N. Forest Park Drive
Peoria, IL 61614-3592

Studies in Art Education: A Journal of Issues and Research in Art Education
National Art Education Association
1916 Association Drive
Reston, VA 22091-1590

Women's Wear Daily
   7 East 12th Street
   New York, NY 10018

Fine Art Publications

African Arts
   The J. S. Coleman African Studies Center
   University of California
   Los Angeles, CA 90024-1310

Afterimage
   Visual Studies Workshop
   31 Prince Street
   Rochester, NY 14607

American Art
   Oxford University Press
   200 Madison Avenue
   New York, NY 10016

American Craft
   72 Spring Street
   New York, NY 10012

Art & Academe
   School of Visual Arts
   209 East 23rd Street
   New York, NY 10023

Art in America
   Brandt Art Publications, Inc.
   575 Broadway
   New York, NY 10012

Art Forum
   65 Bleeker Street
   New York, NY 10012

Arts Hazards News
   Center for Safety in the Arts
   5 Beekman Street
   New York, NY 10018

Art History
   Association of Art Historians
   Basil Blackwell, Ltd.
   108 Cowley Road
   Oxford OX4 1JF
   England

Art Journal
   College Art Association
   275 Seventh Avenue
   New York, NY 10001

Arts Magazine
   P.O. Box 8021
   Syracuse, NY 13217-7952

Art Space
   Ohio Arts Council
   727 East Main Street
   Columbus, OH 43205

Art Week
   12 South First Street
   Suite 520
   San Jose, CA 95113

Ceramics Monthly
  Box 12448
  1609 Northwest Boulevard
  Columbus, OH 43212

Creative Camera
  CC Publishing Battersea Arts Centre
  The Old Towne Hall
  London SW11 5TF
  England

Fiberarts
  50 College Street
  Ashville, NC 28801

Glass Magazine
  647 Fulton Street
  Brooklyn, NY 11217

Hand Papermaking
  Box 10571
  Minneapolis, MN 55458

Image
  Australian Photographic Society, Inc.
  P.O. Box 53
  Hacket, A.C.T., 2062
  Australia

Journal of Aesthetics and Art Criticism
  American Society for Aesthetics
  H-108 Humanities Center
  University of Alberta
  Edmonton, Alberta T6G 2E5
  Canada

Latin American Art
6920 East First Street
Suite 201
Scottsdale, AZ 85251

New Art Examiner
New Art Association
1255 South Wabash
4th Floor
Chicago, IL 60605

New Glass
1850 Union Street, 228
San Francisco, CA 94123

Ornament
1221 South La Cienqa
Box 35029
Los Angeles, CA 90035-0029

Photo Communique
Box 155
Station "B"
Toronto, Ontario M5T 2T7
Canada

Photographer's Forum
Sebin Communications, Inc.
614 Santa Barbara Street
Santa Barbara, CA 93101

Pinhole Journal
Box 1564
Madison Square Station
New York, NY 10159

Raw Visions
  105 Hudson Street
  New York, NY 10013

Red Bass
  Red Bass Productions, Inc.
  2425 Burgundy Street
  New Orleans, LA 70117-7829

Sculpture
  International Sculpture Center
  1050 Potomac Street, N.W.
  Washington, DC 20007

Women's Art Journal
  Women's Art, Inc.
  1711 Harris Road
  Laverock, PA 19118

Employment and Resource Newsletters

Advertising Age
  200 East 42nd Street
  Suite 930
  New York, NY 10017

National Arts Placement Newsletter
  1916 Association Drive
  Reston, VA 22091-1590

USIARTS
  Bureau of Educational and Cultural Affairs
  Room 849
  United States Information Agency
  301 4th Street, S.W.
  Washington, DC 20547

The Washington International Arts Letter
Box 12010
Des Moines, IA 50312

In addition to these employment and resource newsletters, many of the periodicals listed provide useful information related to a wide variety of funding sources and employment opportunities.

PROFESSIONAL ORGANIZATIONS

Advertising Club of New York
  155 East 55th Street
  Suite 202
  New York, NY 10022

American Association of Interior Designers
  1430 Broadway
  New York, NY 10018

American Association of Museums
  1055 Eye Street, N.W.
  Washington, DC 20005

American Association of University Professors
  1012 14th Street, N.W.
  Suite 500
  Washington, DC 20005

American Council for the Arts
  1 East 53rd Street
  New York, NY 10022

American Craft Council
  72 Spring Street
  New York, NY 10012

American Federation of Arts
  41 East 65th Street
  New York, NY 10021

American Institute of Graphic Arts
  1059 Third Avenue
  New York, NY 10021

American Society of Interior Designers
  608 Massachusetts Avenue, N.E.
  Washington, DC 20002-6006

American Society of Magazine Photographers
  419 Park Avenue South
  New York, NY 10016

Art Director's Club of New York
  250 Park Avenue South
  New York, NY 10003

Artists in Print
  Building D
  Fort Mason Center
  San Francisco, CA 94123

Arts International
  Suite 200 L Street, N.W.
  Washington, DC 20026

Arts Management
  408 West 57th Street
  New York, NY 10019

Associated Photographers International
  23024 Ardwick Street
  Woodland Hills, CA 10017

Association of Artist Run Galleries
164 Mercer Street
New York, NY 10013

Association of Hispanic Arts, Inc.
200 East 87th Street
2nd Floor
New York, NY 10028

Association of University Interior Designers
Michigan State University
250 Akers Hall
East Lansing, MI 48824

Biological Photographic Association
6650 Northwest Highway
Suite 112
Chicago, IL 60631

The Canada Council
255 Alberta Street
P.O. Box 1047
Ottawa, Ontario K1P 5UB
Canada

Cartoonists Association
Box 4203 Grand Central Station
New York, NY 10017

Cartoonists Guild
30 East 20th Street
New York, NY 10003

Center for Arts Information
625 Broadway
New York, NY 10012

College Art Association
  149 Madison Avenue
  New York, NY 10016

Color Association of the U.S.
  343 Lexington Avenue
  New York, NY 10016

Designer's Saturday, Inc.
  911 Park Avenue
  New York, NY 10021

Design Management Institute
  621 Huntington Avenue
  Boston, MA 02115

Foundation for Interior Design Education Research
  322 Eighth Avenue
  New York, NY 10001

Governing Board for Interior Design Standards
  341 Merchandise Mart
  Chicago, IL 60654

Graphic Artists Guild
  30 East 20th Street
  New York, NY 10003

Institute of Business Designers
  341 Merchandise Mart
  Chicago, IL 60654

Interior Design Educators Council
  P.O. Box 8744
  Richmond, VA 23226

International Center of Photography
  1130 Fifth Avenue
  New York, NY 10028

International Society of Interior Designers
Design Center Los Angeles
433 South Spring St., Suite 6-D
Los Angeles, CA 90013

National Architectural Accrediting Board
1735 New York Avenue, NW
Washington, DC 20006

National Art Education Association
1916 Association Drive
Reston, VA 22091

National Association of Artists' Organizations
c/o Washington Project for the Arts
400 7th Street N.W.
Washington, DC 20004

National Cartoonists Society
9 Ebony Court
Brooklyn, NY 11229

National Council for Interior Design Qualification
118 East 25th Street
New York, NY 10010

Professional Photographers of America
1090 Executive Way
Des Plaines, IL 60018

Society of American Graphic Artists
1983 Fifth Avenue
New York, NY 10028

Society of Graphic Designers of Canada
  P.O. Box 813
  Adelaide Street East Post Office
  Toronto, Ontario M5C 2K1
  Canada

Society of Illustrators
  128 East 63rd Street
  New York, NY 10021

Society of Photographers and Artists Representatives
  Box 845 FDR Station
  New York, NY 10022

Society of Publication Designers
  60 East 42nd Street
  New York, NY 10165

Southern Arts Federation
  Suite 500
  1293 Peachtree Street, NE
  Atlanta, GA 30309

Technical Association of the Graphic Arts
  1 Lomb Memorial Drive
  P.O. Box 9887
  Rochester, NY 14623-0887

Technical Illustrators Management Association
  P.O. Box 1021
  Inglewood, CA 90308

Type Director's Club
  60 East 42nd Street
  Suite 1416
  New York, NY 10065

Volunteer Lawyers for the Arts
    36 West 44th Street
    New York, NY 10036

WESTAF (Western States Arts Federation)
    236 Montezuma Avenue
    Santa Fe, NM 87501

Women's Graphic Center
    1727 North Spring Street
    Los Angeles, CA 90012